DISASTER RECOVERY AND CONTINUITY OF BUSINESS

A PROJECT MANAGEMENT GUIDE AND WORKBOOK FOR NETWORK COMPUTING ENVIRONMENTS

John L. Cimasi

ISBN: 1453609350
ISBN-13: 9781453609354

The book offers a comprehensive guide for businesses on how to develop and implement effective disaster recovery and continuity of business plans that will make it possible for the company to keep working in the face of an event that cripples its information systems. Useful charts and helpful bulleted lists are offered for planning teams to customize for their company's needs. It's hard to think of any aspect of continuity planning that is not addressed by the book.

The book is well organized and logically structured. The author asked for feedback on whether the repetition of certain ideas for emphasis perhaps crossed into the realm of redundancy, but the editor noted no such effect. The repeated ideas come across more as reinforcement of important concepts and tasks, rather than a revisiting of ground that's already been covered.

Professional, thorough, detail-oriented, and knowledgeable. It's clear to readers that the author has "been there, done that" with developing DR/COB plans and has the voice of experience that can help users of this guide prepare for any eventuality.

— Editor

"Project management activities focus on the end product, understandably so. A project that delivers the end product on time and within budget is considered by some to be a success. Unfortunately, these are not complete indicators of project success. There are many examples of project underutilization, or even project failures, due to inadequate testing, improperly defined business objectives, etc. Insufficient disaster recovery planning is yet another example of a responsibility which frequently suffers from insufficient focus during the PM process. As the author notes, psychological denial of potential failure, insufficient understanding of business needs, inadequate resources, and other factors contribute to the lack of attention to disaster recovery and continuity-of-business planning. The early discussion of impediments is a clear and realistic review of challenges and constraints which are found in all organizations.

Project management life cycle consists of a number of phases, and the author provides considerable details about each step. This depth provides important conceptual and practical guideposts for developing and implementing projects aimed at disaster recovery and continuation of normal business functions in the face of adversity. For example, highlighting the importance of a project sponsor and the project council, describing the benefits of using consultants, delving into details pertaining to communications, and recommendations for conducting effective meetings are all areas where his corporate and organizational background augments theoretical concepts. The material is thus presented at a realistic and fundamental level.

The book focuses on LAN/WAN environments; however the principles, examples, and documents are transferable to many other IT environments. The author notes that the baseline project plan is a living document, revised as a project progresses in order to accommodate changing circumstances. He also addresses many components of projects which are sometimes ignored or given minimal attention. The excitement of completing a project sometimes causes participants to lose sight of critical final phases in the PM life cycle. Proper closure, documentation, and eventual "lessons learned" reflections are essential for ongoing operational tasks. They are also important from the institutional perspective, in that they may inform future projects and decision making.

Feasibility assessments must be undertaken during the early stages of any project. Financial feasibility, while critical, is not the only type of assessment that needs to be performed. The author's practical experience with the nuts and bolts of project development is reflected in the exhaustive lists of recommendations, suggestions, and warnings. The book may thus serve as a handy guide, a checklist, calling attention to other facets of feasibility. These include assessment of technical resources and skill-sets, pitfalls of organizational politics, legal and contractual constraints, challenges of physical site preparedness, identification of mainstream and non-standard tasks, etc.

Stylistically, the author relies on repetition of important topics. This is an effective method for educational purposes — indeed, the book's objective is to educate practitioners about an important topic. The author also includes examples of output from a number of software packages, lists of external resources, and various categorized reference sections. The end result is an informative and persuasive discussion, and a potential guide to an action plan."

Bill Lin, Ph.D.
Chair, Computer Information Systems Department
SUNY Buffalo State College
Buffalo, New York

ABOUT THE AUTHOR

John Cimasi received his bachelor of arts at the State University of New York at Buffalo, certifications in networking and systems analysis and design from SUNY at Buffalo, and a master of science in information technology from Regis University in Colorado.

The author worked as a manager in the information technology industry for over twenty years. During this period, he supervised teams in both small local area and global enterprise networks. The creation, implementation, and maintenance of disaster recovery and continuity of business plans were a major part of the author's professional obligation.

Mr. Cimasi retired in 2008 as a senior vice president, technical infrastructure operations manager for Citigroup, Amherst, New York.

DEDICATION

The author dedicates this book to his wife, Deborah Wollschlager Cimasi. Her enthusiastic support of the author's many quixotic endeavors over the past thirty-six years has earned her an honored place in the pantheon of gracious wives.

In addition, to my remarkable son, Peter John Cimasi, I offer my love, respect, and admiration for his indomitable spirit of adventure, sense of humor and prodigious intellect.

Thanks for contributions from:
Charles Cimasi, MBA
Theresa Ferraro, MSE
Deborah Cimasi
William Lin, PhD
Ronald Rabin, PhD

PREFACE

Over the past four decades, information technology [IT] has provided a tremendous increase in power, knowledge, productivity, and profit to government, academia, private enterprise, and individuals. However, one must view these gains in the context of the vulnerability for failure of these same systems. When failure cannot be an option, planning for the worst becomes prudent "best practice."

This guide sets forth elements of a disaster recovery plan within a classic project management paradigm. This project management approach is useful for organizations and technology support groups wanting to implement an effective disaster recovery [DR] or continuity of business [COB] program.

This guide sets forth elements of a disaster recovery plan within a classic project management paradigm.

As used in this book, disaster recovery [DR] will refer to the information technology component of emergency planning. continuity of business [COB] will refer to the business or client component of the same plan. The two terms are often used interchangeably, and, indeed, there is significant overlap between the two concepts. This is especially the case when DR represents both the IT and business components of recovery planning.

The workbook is written from the perspective of a DR/COB project manager. However, business operations managers will also gain valuable insight into challenges concerning the planning process meant to protect their organizations from the calamity of disaster.

Unfortunately, some internal information technology groups and the organizations they serve do not employ a rigorous approach to the planning and implementation of effective DR or COB schemas. We will explore some of the reasons for insufficient planning later on in the text.

Organizations depending on computers and networking to expedite their business plan are at risk of harmful consequences because of the lack of prudent emergency planning. Often their business plan does not ask, and therefore does not answer, the pertinent questions concerning risk, starting with the phrase, **"What if…?"**

Even with a written strategy, the lack of understanding of basic DR principles, coupled with insufficient attention to proper project planning processes or the availability of sufficient resources, can lead to plan failure.

The question "What if…?" commences the inquiry that leads to effective planning for disaster.

Continuity of business plans written with little regard to the integration of information technology and other dependencies can lead to plan failure as well. It is not good enough for an organization or business to claim the existence of a DR/COB solution without a detailed and tested design that insures the plan's successful implementation.

Another objective of this manual is to provide information technology and business managers with many of the concepts and actual tools leading to the collection and correlation of information to create and implement DR/COB plans for LAN/WAN computing environments. It will not only suggest guidelines but also provide multiple templates, checklists, and examples to commence, organize, and complete a DR/COB project

The book uses a traditional project management "life cycle" paradigm to organize process information. The "life cycle" approach (see figure I) is a proven and effective methodology to bring a plan to fruition from start to finish and back to start again. The project management approach to DR/COB planning necessitates the inclusion of some principals, forms, and checklists related solely to project management. Many of the sample forms are found in chapter 5.

Ideas relevant to the composition of a workable plan are contained within the Design Phase of the project management outline. Called "The Disaster Recovery Cluster of *Rs*," this alliterative list is an amusing way to organize and remember these important concepts.

The reader will undoubtedly become aware of certain repeating concepts in book. The repetition is deliberate and meant to emphasize their importance.

CONTENTS

PREFACE xi

CONTENTS xiii

INTRODUCTION xvii

CHAPTER 1. 1
  Impediments to a Workable DR/COB Plan. 1
  Conceptual Elements of a COB/DR Plan. 4
  Scope and Limitations of this Workbook. 4
  Summary of Chapter 1 5

CHAPTER 2. 7
  PROJECT METHODOLOGY 7
  Pre-engagement Phase 8
  Engagement Phase 8
  Discovery Phase. 11
  Design Phase. 13
  Implementation Phase 20
  Close project and Post-Implementation Phase. 23
  Maintenance phase 24
  Summary of Chapter 2 25

CHAPTER 3................................... **27**
   DR/COB Concepts Associated with a Cluster of "Rs".............27
   Reality..27
   Robustness and Reliability................................28
   Remediable...29
   Redundancy / Replication.................................30
   Resources/Relevant/Reasonable/Right Sized................30
   Reconnaissance...31
   Risk Analysis..32
   Rules and Ramifications..................................35
   Roles/Relegation/Responsibility/Reachable and Reactive...36
   Review/Revise/Rehearse/Refine/Retrain/Refrain Cycle......37
   Readiness/Rapidity/Remoteness............................38
   Reversibility/Restoration/Recuperation/Resumption........41
   Results / Deliverables...................................42
   Summary of Chapter 3.....................................44

CHAPTER 4................................... **45**
   LESSONS LEARNED—OPINION and advice.......................45
   Ethics...45
   Project Approach...46
   Summary of Chapter 4.....................................57

CHAPTER 5................................... **59**
   FORMS AND CHECKLISTS.....................................59
   Redundancy/Replication Checklist.........................59
   Level Three Cost Estimate - Sample Form..................62
   Financial Impact of Failure—basic Form...................64
   Meeting Agenda with Last Meeting Minutes—Sample Form.....65
   Disaster Alert Contact Pyramid Test Guidelines...........66
   Alert Pyramid—Contact Sheet Sample Form..................68
   Alert Pyramid Contact Test Metrics Worksheet.............69
   DR/COB Remote Site planning Form.........................69
   Risk Acceptance for Disaster Plan Deviations Form........75

DR/COB Test Planning Worksheet Form 76
DR/COB Test Results Form 79
Software and application Information Collection Form. 82
User Data Information Collection Matrix Form 83
Multiple Projects Worksheet Sample. 84
Project Planning Template—Sample #1 85
Project Planning Simplest Template—Sample #2 87
Detailed Project Plan template—Sample #3 88
Project Planning Document—Sample #4. 98
Project Planning Milestone Document—sample #5. 101
Partial Construction Checklist for Technical Equipment Areas. 103
Project Completion and Feedback—Sample Form 106
Customer Satisfaction Form for the IT Team. 108
Summary of Chapter 5 109

Definition of Terms **110**

Sources of COB/DR Information **127**

Bibliography and References **129**

Index **131**

INTRODUCTION

Computers that serve as communication and productivity tools drive most business processes today. The ability of computer systems to input, access, manipulate, format, and share data is critical to the economic viability of organizations of all sorts—even countries.

The lack of efficient risk management plans is a problem that leaves organizations vulnerable to costly failure. In most organizations, production loss due to computing or communication failures can be significantly hurtful and even catastrophic to their mission.

Organizations that plan and follow a course of action to design and implement an effective disaster recovery [DR] and continuity of business [COB] plan to address potential information systems failure create forward-looking, risk management solutions to improve situational vulnerabilities.

This workbook will outline an approach for planning, implementation, and maintenance of effective DR/COB plans for those organizations using LAN/WAN computer environments.

It will furnish any information technology team and the organizations it supports with concepts, checklists of concerns, necessary tasks, and other planning tools.

- Bulleted outlines, multiple checklists, forms, and templates will serve a practical need for any project manager that wishes to immediately commence and complete a DR/COB project.
- The inclusion of experiential, real-world observations and advice gives some of the concepts a useful context.

A subordinate but very important goal of this book is to include useful information about project management, leading effective teams, and some basic networking technology concepts. Of these, the formal project management "life cycle" planning methodology is most important.

CHAPTER 1

Impediments to a Workable DR/COB Plan

If a DR/COB plan is so sensible, why would any organizations be found wanting? Some of the following listed impediments to universal implementations of effective COB/DR plans are quite common:

■ Psychological denial: "It can't happen to us"
  □ Of course, it cannot happen until it does happen. That is the time when denial meets regret. Disaster recovery planning is very much like an insurance policy: there is a periodic premium to pay to insure business continuity and insure against catastrophic loss.

■ An absence of detailed understanding about the content and maintenance of an organization's proprietary, critical business processes
  □ Many business managers lack a detailed catalog of critical production processes. This includes process function and process design.
    • Function refers to the process output—what, why, who, when, and where it fits in the hierarchy of business criticality.
    • Design refers to the how it accomplishes the function.

■ Without the understanding of design and function that detailed documentation provides, critical functions become clouded over time—especially if key employees leave.
  □ For example:
    • A DR/COB process document indicating that a particular result is produced when a user clicks on a desktop icon may be insufficient if the process behind the icon is unknown. In a new COB environment, that icon may not exist on the computer monitor, and even if it did, the code may not produce the expected results. The complete process must be known to replicate the desired effect.

- A lack of understanding as to the implications of business process failure
  - ☐ Organizations have different tolerances for "down time." The same is true for various departments within a large organization. It is necessary to analyze every link in the production chain (there may be one or one hundred) to assess any potentially harmful impact if one link breaks.
  - ☐ Always ask the critical DR/COB question "what if." This question should lead to a "cost of failure" metric. When an organization understands the real cost of failure, investment in a COB plan becomes good business practice.

- Insufficient regard for the critical support value of organization or corporate facilities, equipment, data assets, and personnel
  - ☐ It is not prudent for corporate managers to consider the efficient delivery of background services like real estate facility maintenance and information technology to be magical. Managers should not consider the personnel that deliver these services as gnomes that guard the treasure of the organization in secret, coming to the fore only when summoned by a manager with a problem.
  - ☐ The managers of an organization should take the time to understand at least the basic concepts, processes, and devices involved in property, equipment, and data maintenance.
  - ☐ Organization managers, along with the appropriate specialists, should understand the importance to production of different elements in the delivery of these services. This understanding will allow an assessment of the negative impact should one of the elements fail.
    - For example:
      - ○ What is the impact of a file server crash?
      - ○ What is the impact of wide area network failure?
      - ○ What is the impact of any particular PC desktop(s) failure?
      - ○ What is the impact of nonfunctioning air conditioning?
      - ○ What happens if the electronic door locks do not work?
      - ○ How will a network virus infection affect production?
      - ○ How will the business deal with a power outage?

- An absence of complete information about DR and COB requirements and possibilities
  - ☐ Once there is a complete understanding of business processes and the elements of production delivery, a continuity of business plan to safeguard production is possible.
  - ☐ Always view DR/COB technical possibilities in the context of business requirements. Said another way, a return on investment [ROI] calculation must be made to insure that the proposed remedies do not exceed the cost of an actual failure. Plans must be scalable.
  - ☐ The discovery, design, and implementation of a DR/COB plan should be a cooperative effort between the organization's business management and the service organizations responsible for technical support.

■ A scarcity of technical resources to formulate a DR plan

   ☐ Because DR/COB plans can include technical or other kinds of not commonly known information, it may be necessary to engage specialists to build an efficient plan. Resources deployed to get it right the first time around are usually a wise investment.

■ A disconnect between the business and IT departments that disallows integration of the technology disaster recovery plans with business continuity of business plans

   ☐ Disaster recovery often refers to those remedial plans that technical teams put in place to address the failure of networks or network devices. Continuity of business often refers to those remedial plans that the business organization puts in place to ameliorate the impact to production from systems failure.

   ☐ DR and COB plans must be closely synchronized so that all enterprise constituents know their role if calamity should occur.

■ A lack of sufficient management resolve and the necessary resources to allow creation and implementation of an integrated DR/COB plan

   ☐ Engage a decision maker with "purse string" privileges as the sponsor of a DR/COB effort to avoid failure due to lack of resources.

   ☐ For success, management must vest sufficient authority in the project manager to expedite the project.

■ Formulation of "offhand," casual plans that give a false sense of security, but in the end will not work because of false premises

   ☐ A poor plan is worse than no plan at all. This is due to the false sense of well-being that a non-workable plan gives to the stakeholders. In an emergency, an inadequate plan also wastes precious time needed to discover what will work.

■ Failure to test and revise existing plans using a deliberate and cyclical system

   ☐ Test all assumptions to prove that they are effective.

   ☐ Testing is a cyclical paradigm. One makes an assumption, tests the assumption, collects the data, revises the assumption if necessary (lessons learned) and starts the testing cycle all over again.

   ☐ Test constantly from the discovery phase through the design and implementation phases of the project plan.

■ Failure to apply meaningful metrics to the iterations of disaster plan test results

   ☐ Record testing data in a thorough manner.

      • Note negative results for process revision.

      • Collect positive results for plan updates.

      • Both positive and negative test results should be attendant with situational awareness. The result of the test may vary depending on the setting. (e.g., where and when is the process tested?)

      • Investigate all necessary test settings.

■ Failure to systematically update the plan and incorporate "lessons learned"
  ☐ Once testing reveals what works and what does not work, revise the plan to reflect the results. A DR/COB plan is a dynamic document. A dynamic document is one that is changeable in accordance with the needs of the organization at a particular place and time.

■ Failure to constantly train the technical and business staff to work the plan
  ☐ "Don't blame'em, train'em" is an old admonishment that encourages managers to train their staff in the use of disaster plans. Training aligned with plan testing is the best way to make sure that the plan and the personnel working the plan are prepared to succeed.

■ Organizational procrastination that impedes the will to proceed
  ☐ In this situation, the stakeholders understand the need to act but are comfortable with their daily routines. They tend to put change off until tomorrow. Postponement breeds complacency that can lead to danger.

Conceptual Elements of a COB/DR Plan

Topical elements of this guide are associated with considerations subordinate to the alliterative "Clusters of *Rs*" listed below. These *R* words describe concepts, characteristics, and inquiries against which one can compare a nascent DR/COB plan. The reader will find these topics discussed in detail within in chapter 3.

- Reality
- Robustness and Reliability
- Remediable
- Redundancy/Replication
- Resources/Relevant/Reasonable/Right Sized
- Reconnaissance
- Risk Analysis
- Rules and Ramifications
- Roles/Relegation/Responsibility/Reachable and Reactive
- Review/Revise/Rehearse/Refine/Retrain/Refrain Cycle
- Readiness/Rapidity/Remoteness
- Reversibility/Restoration/Recuperation/Resumption
- Results/Deliverables

Scope and Limitations of this Workbook

The scope of this workbook will be limited mostly to disaster recovery concepts focused on the local area network [LAN]. Because local area networks are often connected via wide area networks [WAN] to remote resources, some WAN considerations are also included. However, detailed global enterprise-computing concerns are generally beyond the purpose of this book.

Enterprise-computing solutions must necessarily focus in equal measure on large geographic areas and complex connectivity issues. Included in the consideration of global enterprise DR/COB plans are factors such as foreign languages, governments, complex telephony issues, and diverse WAN computing environments. Some of the aforementioned concerns also exist for enterprise plans contained only within North America. While this book focuses on the local computing environment, some of the information and tools provided may be useful for enterprise plans as well.

Conceptually, one can divide local computing systems into five parts:
- LAN Devices—both physical and logical
- Business/organizational processes with their supporting applications
- Data used by applications and their processes
- Personnel using the system for production
- Personnel supporting the system

Generally, the author will treat vulnerabilities of these five elements conceptually at a relatively high level and limit in-depth recommendations concerning particular computing devices, data structures, and application software.

The same high-level approach will be true for the treatment of human resource issues regarding the potential impact of disasters and disaster plans on personnel. However, the lack of in-depth details regarding human resource issues during a disaster should in no way diminish the importance of this topic.

Summary of Chapter 1

Because COB issues and remedies are usually situational, disaster Recovery/continuity of business project managers will likely find it beneficial to refer to several sources of guidance while formulating a specific COB/DR plan. There are significant topical "off the shelf" information sources offered on the Internet, from booksellers, and from disaster recovery related vendors. Many IT companies sell their software, hardware, and consulting products using COB and DR as a benefit and reason to purchase.

This book will address common DR and COB issues. It will provide checklists of relevant items within the phases of a classic project management plan. In addition, it will provide multiple guides, templates and other forms for the collection of information, Project Management and project tracking.

The resulting effective DR/COB plan will lessen the risk of information technology vulnerabilities and loss of organization production due to most kinds of computer network disaster.

CHAPTER 2

PROJECT METHODOLOGY

It is best to approach disaster recovery and continuity of business plans as deliberate projects, not as a piecemeal or ad hoc undertaking. The plans should be organized and expedited within classic project management life cycle phases. To that end, this chapter will clarify the activities and goals within those phases.

Classic Project Management Phases

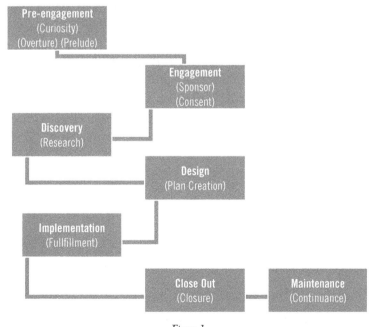

Figure 1

Pre-engagement Phase

Some project management schemas add a Pre-engagement Phase to the project plan. This phase is distinct from the following Engagement Phase because it includes only the very preliminary concepts, concerns, proposals, and decisions concerning the potential of the project.

■ It allows the project proposal to "test the waters" to gauge the level of interest in the organization.

■ During this commencement phase, a vendor or in-house advocate presents a high-level outline defining the basic elements of DR/COB ideas to a decision maker(s).

■ An organization decision maker or project sponsor may initiate the solicitation of vendor(s) via an RFP [request for proposal] to provide information.

■ The idea at this early point in the process is to outline the potential project goals in general terms to determine the level of desirability or feasibility.
  □ For example, to solicit executive staff support, it is common that a vendor and/or project sponsor gives a presentation to stakeholders or executive staff to communicate the features and potential benefits of the project.

In the Pre Engagement Phase, the proposal initiator would surely want to speak or inquire about the potential consequences of not having a good plan in place.

■ Wrapping the justification of a good plan in the mantle of prudence, risk management, and return on investment [ROI] usually makes it more desirable to responsible organization executives.

At the conclusion of the Pre-engagement Phase, the project advocate or project manager should have identified a project sponsor. A sponsor is usually a decision maker with the ability to commit funds. The project advocate would have obtained a commitment to engage the organization for gathering information about the advisability, intent, and other elements necessary before the organization commits to the expense of in-depth Discovery, Design, and Implementation phases of a disaster plan.

Engagement Phase

The Engagement Phase is a continuance of the Pre-engagement phase. With a commitment to explore, the project manager commences a discussion in more detail about the goals of the initiative. The Engagement Phase prepares the way for the in-depth analysis and design of the project.

■ It is important to identify a general idea of the scope and potential constraints of the project so that a feasibility analysis can be started.

- The preliminary feasibility analysis will project preliminarily a wide "Level I" cost estimate (a "guesstimate" sometimes plus or minus 50%) against estimated project returns.

- Preliminary return on investment [ROI] estimates will be an important factor in the decision to proceed or abandon the project idea. (See a simple ROI calculating form in chapter 2 under the "Discovery" heading.)

- During the Engagement Phase, the PM (project manager) must commence looking for staff to help with the Discovery (research) and Design phases of the project.

- Professional temporary help firms marketing consultants with the appropriate systems analysis and design background or DR/COB knowledge experts may be desirable to retain.

- Consultants are sometimes advantageous because:
  - ☐ They work for another firm who is responsible for all employee obligations, including taxes, employment insurance, and benefits.
  - ☐ The personnel are selected based on their subject knowledge and skills.
  - ☐ They are retained at a defined cost for a defined period, making cost projections easier.
  - ☐ Because consultants are temporary help and employed "at will," their service can be discontinued at the end of the project, or indeed any time during the project.
    - Oftentimes these project consultants make excellent permanent employee prospects.

- Make sure the hiring agency fully vets the consultants or temporary-help individuals.
  - ☐ Check their resumes for accuracy.
  - ☐ Call a couple of references they provide.
  - ☐ Insure that the candidates are reputable and will not do damage to the target organization.
  - ☐ Drug testing as well as criminal and credit background checks should be standard procedure.
  - ☐ Include a CNDA (confidential nondisclosure agreement) as a codicil to any agency contract.

Perhaps the most important task of the Engagement Phase is to discover the project "stakeholders" and the formation of the "project council."

- Stakeholders are all of those individuals that the project may use or affect.
  - ☐ For example, a DR/COB project in the big business company might include various internal engineers, vendors, business managers, and departmental user representatives.

- The "project council" should include the above-cited individuals or their representatives.
  - ☐ The project council facilitates communications between the project team and the sponsoring organization.

    □ The project council can also act like a board of directors for the project, providing critical feedback and direction.

■ If the most important task of the Engagement Phase is to discover the stakeholders, one of the most important deliverables is the "communications matrix."
    □ The communications matrix is a list of all of the stakeholders, their role in the project, and their contact information.
    □ The communications matrix is a dynamic document and should be regularly updated and distributed by the project manager.
    □ Consider using e-mail for communications and meeting invitations. E-mail is not only convenient, but the project manager can close the communications loop by requesting a return receipt when the message is read.

■ Still another necessary deliverable in this phase is the setting of the place, time, and agenda of project meetings.
    □ In preparation for every meeting, the PM should provide an agenda that includes a period allotted for each agenda item.
    □ Meandering meetings quickly lose their efficacy.
    □ Start on time; close on time! (See the meeting and agenda templates provided in chapter 5.)
    □ Sometimes, the PM encounters difficulty reaching consensus regarding a convenient time for the meeting. Rule of thumb: do the best you can to get agreement; if it is not forthcoming, set the time and place and expect the participants to adjust their schedules to attend.

■ Properly consider housekeeping chores during the engagement period.
    □ For example, where will the team work, eat, etc.? Procure office space and equipment, including computers and telephones.
    □ Do not forget to start inquiring about any necessary testing and staging areas that will be needed during future project phases.

■ DR/COB projects often include the procurement of real estate, software, equipment, and personnel.
    □ During this phase, discover, compare, and engage vendors for these various purposes.
    □ The PM may be required to send out a general request for information [RFI] to various potential vendors. One or more of the most attractive providers can then be invited to complete an in-depth request for proposal [RFP] with sufficient detail to allow for pricing. After screening and selection, contract negotiations should create a contract to present to management for approval.

■ Last, but very importantly, the engagement period should be a period when a leader [PM] commences team building.

□ Team building as a concept includes all those activities that engage and train personnel to fulfill necessary roles within the team.

□ The sooner a project team can coalesce and commence to work together toward a common goal, the better chance the project has for success.

□ Some team building factors and techniques will be discussed later in the workbook.

■ At the conclusion of the Engagement Phase, the PM should have:

□ A solid commitment by the sponsor to fund at least the upcoming Discovery and Design phases of the project

□ Identified the project stakeholders

□ Completed a communications matrix

□ Formed the project council

□ Put together a Discover and Design team with the requisite space and equipment ready to go to work.

□ Established preliminary meetings (time and place) for staff and stakeholders

Discovery Phase

The Discovery Phase is also called the Definition Phase, the Research Phase, or the Analysis Phase. Regardless of the name, this phase essentially expands the preliminary conceptual work done in the Engagement Phase by diligently ascertaining and recoding business processes and infrastructure toward the goal of stipulating ways to protect them from disaster large and small. During this period, the project team must gather most of the information necessary to construct the project plan [PP] that will lead the team through the Design Phase.

■ Discovery Phase information is usually gathered using some form of interrogation or survey of the relevant target organization's user base—including managers and vendors.

□ Methodologies for this information gathering include both written surveys and interviews.

□ The DR/COB questionnaire in chapter 5 is a helpful tool to gather and organize the necessary data and assist the PM to set a task list with time lines for completion of the Discovery Phase.

Presumably, a relevant subset of the organization's stakeholders will be members of the newly formed project council.

■ The project council is an effective and appropriate venue for this information discovery process.

■ DR/COB planning necessarily includes compiling detailed business requirements, dependencies and risk assessments from all the departments of an organization.

□ Make sure all departments are represented

□ Departments not represented will likely become an impediment to progress

■ As you discover needs and expectations, commence a parallel effort to discover "best practice" solutions.

■ As information is gathered, interpret and collate it within a **"what if"** mind-set.
  ☐ The project team should continue to define the elements (task, time, personnel, money, etc.) that will lead to project "success."

■ Identify quantifiable entities to measure for the purpose of metrics.
  ☐ If you cannot measure a task, assess a risk, or cost a solution, these entities are difficult to use in a determination of the success or failure or the project.

A task list with "Milestones," "Dependencies," "Attribution," "Time Lines," and "Critical Path" items should be starting to form. This should lead to a preliminary scope for the DR/COB project.

Microsoft Project[1] is, for some, a good choice to organize the project. The program allows easy translation from a task list with scheduling to a Gantt chart showing these tasks with their dependencies and time lines visually. MS Project also makes it easy to change project scope should that be necessary—and it usually is necessary. A precedent date change will automatically change subordinate dates. In addition, the program efficiently compiles project performance metrics.

Microsoft Project Task List and Gantt Chart Example

ID	🛈	Task Name	Duration	Start	Finish	Aug '05 17	24	31	07	14
1		**Discovery Phase**	**25 days?**	**Thu 07/28/05**	**Wed 08/31/05**					
2	▦	Create Information Collection For	7 days	Thu 07/28/05	Fri 08/05/05					
3	▦	Form Project Council	2 days	Thu 08/04/05	Fri 08/05/05					
4		Interview Business Heads	10 days	Mon 08/08/05	Fri 08/19/05					
5	▦	Collate Interview information	8 days?	Mon 08/22/05	Wed 08/31/05					

Figure 2 Microsoft product screen shot(s) reprinted with permission from Microsoft Corporation.

There are many other computer software programs in the marketplace that can accomplish the basic housekeeping of project management.

■ An issue with the use of MS Project or other project management application software concerns the lack of general distribution, cost, and usability of a package. If other team members or stakeholders do not own the software, it will be difficult for the PM to communicate.
  ☐ Purchasing a project management program for many people can be expensive.
  ☐ It can take time to develop expertise with project management programs.

---

1. Microsoft Corporation, http://office.microsoft.com/en-us/FX010857951033.aspx.

- One solution to this issue is to build task lists, attributions, and due dates in common programs like Microsoft Excel or Microsoft Word[2]. These documents are much easier to distribute to a diverse population with the expectation that they can be viewed and edited with existing productivity software.

- As an example, please see the DR/COB project tracking template called "DR/COB Sample Site Build Project Tracking Form" in chapter 5.

- A text-based abbreviated project tracking template is also suitable for inclusion in a meeting agenda.

- Use the project council to complete a detailed rendition of the business requirement document [BRD].

- Utilize the information you are gathering about requirements and prices and continue to update the estimate of costs to complete the Design Phase.

Periodically apprise the sponsor or senior management of your progress and request a periodic review the BRD.

- You will be amazed at the important requirement refinements that come forth after successive critical reviews.

- Confirm your funding and seek permission to proceed to the design phase.

- Make sure to forewarn management of any long lead items [LLI] that need to commence immediately but whose final costs are still pending.

- Management never welcomes expensive surprises.
    - ☐ When stipulating expense and time estimates, using ranges instead of absolute numbers is preferable.
    - ☐ Submit expenses and time lines as "goals" so that you have some room to maneuver should impediments crop up.

- For example, please check for an information collection form titled "DR\COB Discovery Questionnaire."

Design Phase

Overview of Design Phase Requirements

- You may need to add appropriate skilled personnel to the design team. There will likely be a continuity of personnel from the Engagement Phase; however, it may be necessary to acquire

---

2.   The reader will find many useful forms and checklists for information gathering and information collation in chapter 5.

other people with special skills, such as realty services, architecture, and various types of LAN/WAN engineering.

- The PM should formalize the coordination of the DR/COB implementation planning and design with other organizational partners, such as the project council.

- Sometimes, if the information technology team or an outside consultant is managing the overall project, the project council may want to appoint a senior manager as a single point of contact to represent their organization and help them track events.

- *Effective, regular communication among stakeholders is among the most important rules to remember. (You will read this advice several times in the workbook.)*

- If remote sites are required for the DR/COB plan, you may need to engage real estate (property) services. The real estate procurement, either leased or purchased, is usually a long lead item [LLI].

- Other LLIs may include engineering schematics, architectural drawings, telephony circuitry, additional electric power, and equipment purchases.
    - ☐ The PM and the project team should identify long lead items with attendant delivery time lines as quickly as possible.
    - ☐ Keep in mind that additional electric power may be needed to accommodate test machines, additional servers, and other equipment necessary to complete the project.
    - ☐ Even if size, numbers, and other details are not yet completely known, start to investigate and compare vendor contacts, capabilities, prices, and other relevant expectations.
    - ☐ Keep management appraised.

- Keep in mind that equipment and software licenses for any DR/COB sites must be purchased. You will need an inventory system.

- Do not forget the need for physical and logical security planning if your organization handles confidential information or has other needs for outside and inside facilities protection.

- It may be necessary to arrange for a moving service and temporary help to do preliminary unskilled work.

- Keep in mind that the installation of equipment requires an appropriate space to "stage" implementation activity.
    - ☐ This includes, among other considerations, room for equipment delivery, un-boxing, operating system/application builds, and staff working space.
        - • The unboxing creates a lot of trash.
            - ○ Plan for disposal.

- If you are purchasing new equipment for the remote DR/COB site, do not forget to insure and track the shipment.

□ Always check incoming inventories against shipment invoices.
- Open at least some of the similar boxes and all of the unique boxes.
  - ○ The time it takes to check will be much less than the time and hassle should some piece of equipment be missing.

□ Maintain a dynamic inventory document that indicates:
- The numbers and kinds of equipment
- Proof of all software licenses
- When the equipment came into the facility
- Where the equipment was deployed
- When the equipment was deployed
- Dates of inventory check and the initials of the checker

The essential nature of the Design Phase is to propose, test, redesign, and test again in a repetitive manner until all design elements are proven successful.

■ Remember that while organizations must usually consider protecting major business functions first, smaller unique ("one-off") departmental tasks must also be identified and included in the plan.

□ Because they do not fit the general departmental mold, so-called one-off tasks that are part of the production process are usually more challenging to support than mainstream tasks.
- Sometimes these nonstandard processes are legacy routines using obsolete technology. Part of your DR/COB plan may be to upgrade one-offs.

■ Testing the design is *not* optional.

□ Departmental "test beds" are laboratory-style facilities that contain an accurate representation of the DR/COB environment.
- The DR/COB environment should emulate the production environment as closely as possible.
- The DR/COB test bed includes computers, software, data, and connectivity elements that, when used by departmental users, prove that the eventual DR/COB site will be effective.

□ The use of test beds as proof of concept is an absolute necessity to insure successful implementation of your design.

■ Identify LAN/WAN needs.

□ While the organization may work fine while serviced by a local area network, that does not mean that applications will work or data will be available over a wide area network.
- Usually the LAN throughput is many times as great as the bandwidth of a WAN circuit. If remote facilities are used for DR/COB purposes, the test beds must be exercised from those locations.

■ If there is a replicated production data set at a COB site for use in an emergency, it is fine to use these data or representative (dummy) data sets.

  ☐ The use of alternate, nonproduction (dummy) data is fine for preliminary testing but is not a valid COB test.

   • Working on alternate data sets does not prove that production can be maintained from the primary data.

   • Intermediate testing with dummy data sets works only for "proof of concept."

  ☐ To achieve "real world" testing, you may have to revise drive mappings and/or disconnect the WAN link from the COB site to the primary site during the test to insure that the COB processes work independently and can access remote resources.

  ☐ Ultimately, actual production must be accomplished to be certain that the remote or alternate DR/COB system actually works.

■ COB exercises must test different disaster levels, ranging from minor outages to the presumption that the primary site has been destroyed.

While designing DR/COB solutions, remember that the sponsoring organization may only require a critical subset of its operational processes replicated at a remote facility. Indeed, only a subset of critical operations may need to be preserved, remote site or not.

■ Do not do any more testing than is necessary to preserve the integrity of the business process. DR/COB exercises are disruptive and expensive to conduct.

■ Work closely with your clients to insure that replicated data sets and other DR/COB processes are appropriately updated after every change in the environment.

■ Pay special attention to the existence and avoid the use of two "primary data sets."

  ☐ Only one file can be primary at a time.

  ☐ There must be a plan to synchronize any data changes from COB backup data sets to the "primary data set" at the primary site.

The Design Phase must use the information gleaned from the Discovery Phase to triage the importance of various production functions and design a phased approach to the COB plan.

■ The emergency response coordinators should have well-thought-out, "first things first" severity choices ready when they declare an emergency.

■ As your plan design progresses, prepare more precise cost estimates.

  ☐ If necessary, revise the return on investment analysis for the client. Constantly ask the question: "**is it worth it?**"

   • It is not uncommon for all users to claim that their process is extremely important. The organization's management must vet the level of process importance in the light of continuity of business cost.

  ☐ Maintain a minimalist mind-set: "**is it really necessary?**"

- For example, perhaps you need not relocate all of the workers in case of the original facility's destruction or disability.
    - ☐ Depending on the amount of time required to rehabilitate the original environment, perhaps only a percentage of an organization's workers are needed to keep the organization operational.

- Likewise, compare alternate methodologies, equipment, and technologies.
    - ☐ Clarify for stakeholders the features, benefits, and potential impact of various plan versions on the organization's ability to survive **different levels** of catastrophe.
    - ☐ Pay attention to the probability that any particular disaster scenario will not be the most catastrophic that can be envisioned during disaster recovery planning.

- In any selected COB/DR schema, client tasks and responsibilities belonging to different phases of the plan are important to define.
    - ☐ Negotiate the details of these phased plan obligations with the appropriate user community or department.

- A paramount obligation of management is to "declare" to the user base that an emergency exists. It is also management's responsibility—albeit usually with consultation among the stakeholders, to invoke a particular segment or level of the DR/COB plan.
    - ☐ Publish the agreement of obligations to declare.
    - ☐ Publish definitions of different severities of disaster.
    - ☐ Get a signature of acceptance from appropriate managers.
    - ☐ Periodically rehearse the declaration of different severities of disaster and the obligation stipulated in the agreement.

- Train the COB business or production workers to fulfill their obligations under the plan.

- Train the information technologists to fulfill their obligations.

- Test the users and information technologists against the plan to insure integration and compliance.

- Gather metrics of the activities and keep a scorecard.
    - ☐ Analyze anomalies and write down lessons learned.

- Incorporate lessons learned into a revised plan.

- Test the revised plan.

COB/DR implementations are oftentimes very much like managing a computer user migration to a new office or operations site. Issues like **"hot cutovers"** versus operational migration to **"parallel computing environments"** come to the fore and must be resolved quickly to allow for proper planning.

■ Hot cutovers are those migration designs where there is only one set of either desktops, servers, or other elements of the LAN infrastructure.

    ☐ In the case or a hot cutover, all of the necessary equipment must move from the original place or be procured and installed in the new production environment in close time proximity with moving the users.

    ☐ Remember that production usually cannot occur during the time it takes to accomplish a hot cutover.

        • Partial production may be possible if the cutover is done in phases over a time period.

■ To lessen the negative effect on productivity, the actual moves should take place during non-working hours.

■ Consider unnecessary hot cutovers as undesirable and dangerous.

    ☐ These seemingly simple plans are fraught with risk.

    ☐ They cannot be rigorously tested.

    ☐ There is no second chance.

    ☐ They may save the organization money in the short term, but oftentimes the complex transfer of device, user, application, data, and connectivity must occur on a compressed time frame.

    ☐ Hot cutovers carry a risk for failure.

■ Indeed, in the case of DR/COB, hot cutovers may simply not be possible. It may be likely that some part of the original infrastructure is destroyed and not available to transplant.

■ To be prudent, the organization should support a parallel production environment.

A "**parallel build**" user migration to a completely predeployed and prepared site—similar or duplicate to the original environment—is the much-preferred method of transitioning workflows from one place to another for DR/COB or other reasons.

■ A parallel build methodology requires either a facility with tested and operable contingency equipment waiting for an emergency (**dark space**) or a place where users can go and supplant other users performing less critical functions.

■ If properly designed parallel build migrations have been rigorously pretested, the move process should approach zero defects.

    ☐ Because equipment and applications have been preinstalled and tested at leisure, only people and the current data set need to arrive at the new destination in a timely manner.

Do not overlook personnel matters:

■ How will the personnel with necessary work-related materials get there?

■ Does the plan include provisions for room, board, and reasonable personal accommodations, such as periodic liaison with families?

■ Understand any union or other contract restrictions or requirements.
 ☐ If your organization has a union representing some or all of the workers, make sure that union representatives are on your stakeholder lists.

■ Putting yourself personally in the context of different levels of disaster can help to lead you to a list of potential personnel concerns.

■ As always, testing your assumptions will undoubtedly add to the list of personnel concerns.

If you use either a parallel or hot cut migration technique for DR/COB remote site migration planning, a high bandwidth data link from the original site to DR/COB location, allowing for bit-level replication of data, is a good idea.

■ Be aware of data recovery challenges when primary data sets are destroyed.
 ☐ Real-time bit-level replication of data to the COB site avoids the daunting task of data recovery from backup tapes or having to deal with replicated data that is not up to date.

■ If an IT team needs to restore an entire "server farm" from DR tape backups, the recovery time will be dependent on:
 ☐ The amount of data to be recovered
 ☐ The existence and availability of a similar tape machine
 ☐ The time to procure new servers
 ☐ The time it takes to rebuild data directories
 ☐ The transfer throughput from the tapes to the new servers

■ If the same model of tape machine is not readily available, its procurement and setup will add significantly to the restoration.
 ☐ Large companies sometime have similar machines at different sites. However:
  • These different sites may be put in jeopardy if their backup machines are deployed to service data restoration from another site.
  • The destroyed tape machine may be obsolete and another not available.
  • Newer machines may not have compatible software and hardware to read the backup tapes.
  • Check for availability of a duplicate tape machine for data recovery purposes.
  • Test restoration of data on the alternate machine.

■ Many experts in the information technology business understand that a large data set restoration from a backup tape could take weeks to months. You must plan accordingly.
 ☐ In light of the potentially slow recovery with tape backups, it is a good idea to use the above-mentioned high bandwidth data link to back up critical files to a preexisting server at the COB site.

☐ If a real-time, bit-level, data replication procedure is in place, the users should be able to more or less sit down at a machine connected to the alternate DR/COB LAN/WAN and go to work.

■ Alternatively, COB users may use remote access technology to access their applications and data at the DR/COB site via an Intranet WAN link or perhaps even via the Internet from home.

■ The final disaster design plan should schedule an orderly deployment.

☐ Management will likely want the transfer of production to be done as soon as possible. Be cautious about their expectations concerning the number of users that can be deployed during a particular time period. Do not promise what you cannot deliver.

☐ Keep in mind that production workers deployed to the COB site must have IT support.

  • The need for "business as usual" [BAU] support will split your team.

    ○ Plan accordingly for sufficient staffing.

■ The final design should delegate project tasks and duties to personnel trained to work the DR/COB plan to a successful conclusion.

■ The final design should answer all of the "what if" concerns that the project manager, the project team and the project council have identified.

■ When the design plan is completed, tested, and declared workable by the project team, the project manager should present it to senior management for approval.

■ Upon presentation of the plan design, it may be appropriate to ask management to make funding available for the **implementation and maintenance** of the plan.

☐ Management may or may not want the design project team to implement or maintain the plan. Implementation and maintenance of the plan sometimes require skill sets not possessed by the design team.

■ BACK OUT PLAN

☐ Every action item that might affect production should have a corresponding "Back-Out Plan." The Back-Out Plan stipulates what should be done in the case of disaster plan item failure.

☐ It is usual for Back-Out Plans to stipulate a procedure to restore the affected environment to its original configuration.

Implementation Phase

The Implementation Phase involves the execution of the DR/COB Design Phase plan. Answer the following questions:

☐ Has the necessary equipment been delivered for deployment?

☐ Did you prepare sufficient storage and "staging" space?

☐ Has responsibility for all of the implementation tasks been delegated?

☐ Have all of the delegated tasks been given a time line for completion?

☐ Has appropriate authority and resources been granted to individuals tasked with things to accomplish?
  - RECAP:
    - **There is nothing as inefficient and frustrating as the demand for productivity from people that do not have the resources or authority to do the job.**

☐ Has the authority, decision, or management organization hierarchy been flattened as much as possible?
  - There should be as few **"hub and spoke"** decision bottlenecks as possible.
    - Hub and spoke organizations require that subordinates request permission for all activities from a central manager.
      - Hub and spoke organizations waste time and effort.
      - Hub and spoke organizations increase risk because subordinates are prohibited from acting independently and immediately to address time-sensitive tasks.
  - Empower and trust your team. Let members deal with one another with a minimum amount of constraint.
    - Keep organization management informed.

☐ Do **organizational silos** have sufficient cross-functional communication?
  - Organizational silos are essentially hub and spoke arrangements that are stacked very high within functional or management boundaries. Unfortunately, unless great care is taken, information goes up and down the silo and often is trapped within.
    - A dedicated and periodic effort must be made to tap and gather appropriate information within the silos for sharing with the entire organization.

☐ Are results being tracked and metrics recorded and compiled?
  - Are goals being met within planned time frames?

☐ RECAP:
  - Do subordinates possess sufficient resources to achieve their tasks?

☐ Are you guarding yourself and your subordinates against burnout?
    - Burnout can occur especially quickly when individuals responsible for **deliverables** do not have the authority or resources to complete the task on target.
    - Frustration is a major cause of burnout.

☐ RECAP:
- Does the project manager (PM) appropriately view himself as a resource to the team?
- Does the PM demonstrate an attitude reinforcing the idea that one of her most important functions is to serve the subordinates on the team?

☐ RECAP:
- Is the team performing the project life cycle (test/implement/revise/test) for each relevant task or deployment?

☐ Are users being trained to use the new environment?
- The Human Resources Department is often a good resource for training needs.
- Training must be done periodically to insure new employees understand the COB plan and to reinforce long-term employees' memories.

☐ Are you communicating progress and problems to the project council?
- Are the members of the project council keeping their management sponsors up to date?

☐ Does the compilation of activity measurements in the Implementation Phase follow the metric assumptions first created in the Discovery Phase?
- If not, why not? Are you missing something?

☐ Are you keeping a "lessons learned" diary?
- Are you actively using these lessons learned to revise the plan via the project life cycle paradigm?

☐ Are you unflappable during stressful times?
- There is no place in project management or a disaster situation for screaming, hollering, or throwing tantrums. **Things inevitably go wrong. When they do, lower your voice, listen, and, most importantly, stay calm and positive.**
- Do not hide from problems. Make yourself visible to your team and clients in times of difficulty. It is the PM's job to garner information and resources efficiently and to solve problems as they come up. Your deportment must be professional at all times. You should manage the deportment of others by your example.

☐ Have you begun to interview and hire for operational maintenance personnel?

☐ Have you begun to train operational maintenance personnel to manage the new environment of implementation?

☐ Have you distributed a customer satisfaction survey to your users? (See chapter 5.)

Close Project and Post-Implementation Phase

When the DR/COB project is successfully implemented, the job is not yet finished. The PM has the responsibility to erase the footprint created for the project and help to set up staff and procedures to maintain the plan.

☐ Review the Customer Satisfaction Survey and collate the metrics.
  • Satisfaction surveys are a great way to learn what was right and wrong from the perspective of workers and management.

☐ Complete any tasks identified by the client survey as unsatisfactory or incomplete.

☐ Prepare a checklist of tasks necessary to support the maintenance of the system.

☐ Review the overall project for lessons learned to be used in future projects.

☐ Finalize the project metrics report.
  • Was the plan successful—on goals, on time, and on budget?
    ○ If not, do you understand why not?

☐ Prepare a new metrics schema for the Maintenance Phase.

☐ Archive relevant records.
  • Save project records, including but not limited to:
    ○ Project planning documents
    ○ Minutes of meetings
    ○ Budgets
    ○ Permissions to proceed
    ○ Satisfactory goal completion signoff documents
    ○ Invoices, including vendor information
    ○ Communication documents, including e-mail

☐ Create and distribute the **process control manual [PCM]**.
  • The PCM elucidates all aspects of the DR/COB plan and stipulates complete procedures for supporting the LAN environment after implementation.

☐ Finalize the project cost accounting report and present it to management.

☐ Obtain a project acceptance signoff from the client management, confirming satisfaction with the successful conclusion of the project implementation.

☐ Cancel whatever items and services specific to the project that you set up at the beginning.
  • In other words, erase the project implementation "footprint."

☐ Do not forget to turn off phones, change keys, return or redeploy computers, etc.

☐ Do your best to find superfluous implementation team members other employment.

☐ Complete the process of personnel terminations, if any.

Maintenance Phase

☐ Hire or arrange to hire the technical team manager and the maintenance team.
- The maintenance team may not be the same personnel that worked to implement the COB/DR project.
- Do special arrangements need to be made for "break and fix services," or will the existing IT team take the responsibility?
- Sometimes the existing primary site IT team or perhaps a vendor will take over the management of the remote site.
- Regardless of the team, it must accept the discipline of testing and maintaining the plan documented in the process control manual [PCM].
- If the ongoing maintenance staff is different from the project implementation staff, has training and a transfer of lessons learned been completed?

☐ Procure offices, maintenance team space, equipment, etc., for the new maintenance team.
- A large room containing a three-sided "bullpen" arrangement to seat the maintenance technicians and their computers works great. It facilitates communication between various members of the team.
- Space should be made on the "bullpen" counter for printers and other office equipment.
- It is very efficient to include shelving to hold spare parts within this same space.
- Do not forget to provide table space for technicians to repair broken machines.
- Remember to provide physical security, such as door locks, to protect the equipment in the room from theft.

☐ Is there a system for users to request technical services, such as **adds, moves and changes,** or **break/fix service** for both application and equipment?
- If the organization is large enough, specialized software that can create a service queue is very efficient.
- Department "**restacks**" (moves) are common in organizations.
  ○ Determine how many moves require a formal project with dedicated resources.

☐ Have you implemented and regularized an operations maintenance efficiency metrics system?
- You should never stop assessing team performance.
- Have you formatted reports that meet management needs?
- Distribute **satisfaction surveys** to the user community, and use them in your maintenance metrics system.

- ○ A Web site is a great way to accomplish satisfaction surveys.
- ○ Whether a Web site is used or not, automate the process to send out surveys to any user receiving service within a particular period.

Summary of Chapter 2

The Methodology Chapter contains DR/COB information that clarifies the goals and activities of a DR/COB project within classic project management phases. The section explains how to engage, define, design, implement, and maintain DR/COB projects using classic project management concepts and phases.

For effective outcomes, it is best to approach disaster recovery and continuity of business plans as complex projects, with organizational process and technical knowledge experts and competent project management creating formal project plans.

As cited at the top of this chapter, for many organizations, the most fail-safe DR/COB schema for a production environment is the opportunity for parallel processing at existing alternate sites. This includes insuring that there are trained personnel and appropriate equipment, software, and connectivity in place that can be assigned on a timely basis to expedite the processes discontinued by the disaster.

CHAPTER 3

DR/COB Concepts Associated with a Cluster of "Rs"

Words That Represent the Substance of a Workable Plan

■ *The Cluster of Rs is a didactic attempt by the author to arrange DR/COB concepts under descriptive, easily remembered words all starting with R.*

■ *The Cluster of Rs is concepts that you need to consider when designing your DR/COB plan*
   □ Reality
   □ Robustness and Reliability
   □ Remediable
   □ Redundancy/Replication
   □ Resources/Relevant/Reasonable/Right Sized
   □ Reconnaissance
   □ Risk Analysis
   □ Rules and Ramifications
   □ Roles/Relegation/Responsibility/Reachable and Reactive
   □ Review/Revise/Rehearse/Refine/Retrain/Refrain Cycle
   □ Readiness/Rapidity/Remoteness
   □ Reversibility/Restoration/Recuperation/Resumption
   □ Results/Deliverables

Reality

□ Does a parallel production facility exist?
   • Most other continuity preparations assume that personnel will survive the disaster. Unfortunately, survival of workers is never assured.

- ○ Therefore, for many organizations, **the only totally fail-safe DR/COB schema for a critical production environment is parallel production processing at existing alternate sites with existing alternative personnel.**
  - ▪ This plan includes insuring that there are trained personnel, appropriate equipment, and tested processes in place that can be assigned on a timely basis to replace those processes discontinued by the disaster.

Robustness and Reliability

☐ Is the present computing system robust and reliable, so that there is rarely a need to invoke a disaster recovery plan?

- • The reliability of the primary LAN infrastructure, including equipment data and application structures, is paramount in importance. Local or remote DR/COB plans may never need to be used if the original environment is sufficiently robust and reliable.
  - ○ Money invested today on the "best of breed" equipment, combined with the "best practice" builds and maintenance of physical and logical systems, proves to be inexpensive in the end.
- • Many major technology vendors offer information and solutions to meet the challenge of reliability. Hewlett Packard, Sun, Network Appliance, EMS, and IBM are among many technology companies that supply systems possessing disaster prevention technology.
  - ○ For example, in an article from Market Wire titled "IBM and Network Appliance Relationship Delivers New Product Offerings for Small and Medium-Sized Businesses" (August 2, 2005), the following blurb suggests a partnership that delivers robust data storage reliability.

    "The IBM TotalStorage N3700 is a robust NAS solution scaling up to 16 terabytes designed to deliver the ease and functionality of Internet Protocol attached storage along with the pervasiveness of iSCSI SAN technology. It offers features and functions SMB customers value, including support for disaster recovery, which allows users to mirror data both within the appliance as well as to a remote device."[3]

    - ▪ In the case cited above, NAS [Network Attached Storage] data mirroring to a remote SAN [storage area network] device would likely be sufficient to make unnecessary the need for local backup tapes. File server and LAN throughput, along with the bandwidth of the WAN circuits between remote devices, are factors to consider when considering data backup.

---

3.   "IBM and Network Appliance Relationship Delivers New Product Offerings for Small and Medium-Sized Businesses," Bloomberg.com, Market Wire, August 2, 2005, http://quote.bloomberg.com/apps/news?pid=conew sstory&refer=conews&tkr=IBM:US&sid=a54BJK_AMex4.

☐ Are reliability protections, such as antivirus software and firewalls, installed as a bulwark against hacking and data theft or corruption?

  ○ Technology managers all too often overlook defensive preparations against the usual and obvious dangers of the day. As stipulated above, the best offense is a good defense.

  ○ Most disasters are avoided if IT teams start with good equipment, effective software, and do those mundane day-by-day tasks that protect the environment.

☐ When adapting proactive and effective "risk management" guidelines, has the organization's investment in robust and reliable equipment and processes been developed or purchased with the underlying rationale of prudence and cost effectiveness?

  • Assess the value of the protected process against the cost to provide a certain level of disaster preparedness. Establish an ROI rational.

☐ Will omissions in the plan be interpreted as malfeasance?

  • Malfeasance means that you should have known better or did know better but neglected to provide an effective plan, thereby causing damage to the organization.

    ○ If you are the responsible party for planning a disaster defense, it is necessary to insure that your analysis and design reach a level of reasonable professionalism that will perform the expected recovery and save the company.

    ○ Said another way: all reasonable effort must be made to identify all business risks and design a complete solution for disaster recovery and continuity of business. Do not ignore anything of consequence. Do always ask "what if?"

  • A defense against the risk of criticism lies in diligent communication and cooperation with the production managers. Get their signed agreement as to the efficacy of any plan.

Remediable

☐ Is the present computing system easy to remediate so that a remote disaster recovery plan may not be necessary?

  • Part of the robustness and reliability of a system is the ability to remediate or fix the equipment in a timely manner if it fails.

  • Technical support organizations should consider the efficacy of storing spare parts and/ or establishing relationships with vendor partners that can respond quickly if a simple equipment or application failure affects production.

  • Major equipment manufacturers and retailers often provide an overnight or courier service to replace defective critical equipment.

  • Be aggressive about contacting manufacturers to inquire about anomalies with their devices. It is a good idea to subscribe to manufacturers' support plans. Again, compare the cost of this support to the importance of the processes the device supports.

- A good maxim is, "The best DR/COB planning is systems planning that makes unnecessary the need for a DR/COB plan."

Redundancy / Replication

☐ Is the present system redundant?
- **HAVE YOU IDENTIFIED AND REMOVED SINGLE POINTS OF FAILURE?**
- Referring to the saying that "the best defense is a good offense," IT managers heeding the concept of computing environment robustness and reliability will seek out and remove any single point of failure in their LAN/WAN environments. They will do their best to convince management that it is prudent to invest in redundant hardware, redundant circuits, and other redundant system elements to avoid chokepoints that can lead to system failure.
  - ○ Some of the "single points of failure" to look for are listed in the Redundancy/Replication Checklist in chapter 5.

☐ Are the software programs and data stores replicated?
- As we have applied the concept of redundancy to physical resources, replication of software applications and data stores is a similar concept that is applicable to all logical resources.
- Devices such as tape backup systems and storage area networks [SANs] with data mirroring are indispensable to insure preservation of information resources in case of a system failure.
- Do not stop at application data replication. Insure that operating systems and emulator session files as well as switch and router configuration files are readily available for restoration.

Resources/Relevant/Reasonable/Right Sized

☐ Are there sufficient resources, both monetary and technical, to plan, implement, invoke, and maintain a DR/COB plan?
- "One cannot make a silk purse from a sow's ear" is an old adage that is instructive. To make a DR/COB plan come to fruition, the PM needs resources such as authority, expertise, staffing, space, and money. Perhaps the most important factor of all is the management commitment to provide sufficient resources to allow the DR/COB plan to manage potential risks to the organization.

☐ Are the stipulated DR/COB resources relevant and right sized appropriately for the organization?

- The concept of "right sizing" is consequential. A DR/COB plan that is prudent for a company like a large global bank may not be sensible for a small attorney's office. The project manager, in consultation with the organization's management, must match the risk of productivity loss against the complexity and expense of the disaster plan.
  - In some organizations, the only disaster plan that is reasonable and relevant may consist only of a simple data backup and a couple of extra PCs.

☐ Are the DR/COB costs reasonable on an ROI basis? Is the economic risk not worth the effort and investment?

- "Right sizing" is the basis for return on investment [ROI]. When one compares the disaster risk to business production in dollars, the project manager and organization management can calculate the range of investment suitable for DR/COB plans.
- Figure 3 is a very basic Microsoft Excel template for calculating ROI.
- One can easily expand this template to accommodate more details.
- Derive "opportunity cost" (profit not made is profit lost!) estimates via the engagement and discovery process.
- Indicate an estimated percentage range of accuracy before submitting the form to management.

Disaster Recovery / Continuity of Business
RETURN ON INVESTMENT CALCULATION TEMPLATE

Expense Item(s)	Estimated Cost	Estimated Hard $ Return	Estimated Opportunity $ Return	Subtotal $ Return
				$0
				$0
		$0	$0	$0
				$0
	Total Estimated Cost	Total Hard $ Return	Total Opportunity $ Return	Total $ Return
	$0	$0	$0	$0

Figure 3

Reconnaissance

☐ Is there a system in place to forewarn of impending outage? Does this system alert the necessary personnel in the case of system failure?

- Is there a methodology for response to system alerts?
  - Forewarning of an impending system failure sometimes allows an opportunity to fix or adjust to the problem before production is lost.

- Is the alert system automated or manual?
  - The convenience of an accurate and automated system cannot be overstated. Manual systems require a disciplined approach by the technical maintenance team.
- If the alert system is manual, is there a procedure to check it periodically?
- Is the response modality in either case of alarm robust or fail-safe?
- Does the staff understand the meaning of alerts and the implication of various breakdowns?
  - Is periodic reconnaissance training scheduled?
- Combine system monitoring with a **process control manual [PCM]**.
  - A PCM is a document that lists and explains all system maintenance procedures in detail. This instruction manual is necessary to aid in training staff. It also insures that consistent best practice is maintained across the IT organization.

Risk Analysis

☐ Was a business impact analysis completed? (See appendix.)
- A business impact analysis includes a valuation of processes deemed critical or worthy of inclusion in a DR/COB plan.
- Questions about management expectations regarding production "down time" are necessary for those processes considered vital to the business.
- Put in other words, the PM must discover (usually done during the Discovery Phase of the project plan) how long the organization can sustain loss of production for any of the many processes that constitute the daily production workflow.

☐ Complete a "gap analysis" to determine the correct elements and actions necessary to get from plan deficiency to compliance. A good source to learn about a gap analysis tool is the Praxium Research Group Ltd. Web site.[4]
- A gap analysis defines the present situation and compares it to the desired result or end state. If there is a "gap," the analyst should identify activities or impediments on the path to closing the gap. A plan for success results from the comparisons. Identifying necessary "means to an end" tasks and solving any obstructing issues will lead to the desired result.
- Discover ideas that point the way to success by conducting brainstorming sessions (Design Phase) with knowledge experts. Use these action ideas to move the deficits to a desired result.
- Subsequently, compose a corrective action plan [CAP] with specific tasks, time lines, and personnel attributions.
  - Follow up to insure completion of assignments.
- Create a metric score card to track progress.

---

4.   ISO 9001 2000 Gap Analysis Tool, Praxium Research Group Ltd., http://www.praxiom.com/iso-gap.htm.

☐ Manage the corrective action plans (CAP).

- Aggressively address the issues, attribute action items to appropriate knowledge experts or task managers, and set time lines for issue resolution. If the time to resolution is of paramount importance, one can declare that time is of the essence.

☐ Classify **risk level** for infrastructure, device, processes, and data risk.

- Risk level refers to the effect of a disaster on each production process. It stipulates an item's value to the organization.
  - ○ Consider risk level when calculating return on investment in your DR/COB plans.
  - ○ Ignore items that have no value and, therefore, have little risk.
- For simplicity, one might categorize items as high, medium, or low risk.
  - ○ If you desire more detail, use a Likert scale[5] type of numeric chart. This scale is helpful to provide visual representation of risk levels from one to ten for each vital process identified.
- Observe that the classifications of some items are inclusive of others.
  - ○ For example, if a file server holds high-risk data, then the file server itself must also be classified as high-risk. If the server is high risk, then the network is high risk, etc.
  - ○ The entire networking infrastructure must be classified as high as the highest-risk device it connects.
  - ○ For example, the **risk chart** should cascade as shown below from the more detailed to the more general.

---

1. **If information [data] risk level is high**
    a. **Servers where data resides risk level is high**
        i. **Infrastructure risk level or security classification level where the servers live is high**

☐ Considerations for taking data off-site The Redundancy/Replication section in the workbook identifies the wisdom of data backups.

- If DR/COB full data backups are stored off-site, as they should be, insure that your tape logging, security, and transport methodologies are reliable. For example:
  - ○ Who transports the tapes?
    - ▪ Is the transport agent reliable and bonded?
  - ○ Where will the tapes be stored?
    - ▪ Is the environment secure and climate controlled?
    - ▪ Is the tape cabinet fireproof?
    - ▪ Can the tape cabinet be locked?

---

5.   A Likert scale is often used in questionnaires that want to elicit a level of agreement with a particular entity.

- ○ Keep on-site logs of cycled tapes in both the primary and storage sites.
  - Tape storage logs should, at minimum, contain the following information:
    - Date in
    - Tape number
    - Original date tape used
      - ○ Tapes should not be used more than a few times or for more than a couple of years
    - Date recycled to primary site
    - Date destroyed
- ○ Is there an efficient methodology for recovering particular tapes from the storage facility?
  - Is there a data directory to indicate which files are on which tapes?
  - Can the users use the data dictionary to discover where or if a file exists?
  - How does a user ask for a "file restore"?
- ○ Are all transported data encrypted?
  - Unencrypted data, if intercepted by inappropriate persons, may pose a material financial risk to a business. In the least, it can lead to a public relations disaster.
  - No important data should be allowed to leave the primary site unencrypted.
    - This rule includes important business data on laptops or other mobile devices.
  - If the encryption algorithm requires a password to access the data, insure that the passwords are kept in at least a couple of secure places.
    - Never entrust the password to only one person. Have at least two persons with the ability to decrypt the data.
      - ○ Trusted employees sometimes leave and refuse or are unable to communicate critical information.
    - Some corporations require two sets of two people, each group with one-half of the password.
      - ○ While this "half double-double" password system safeguarding system is a bit cumbersome, it is very secure, and it is very likely that the company will have at least two employees with different halves of the password.
- Are the data on the tapes randomly tested on a periodic basis for integrity?
  - ○ Ignore this periodic testing at your great peril!
  - ○ Regular recovery of files from the backup tapes is sufficient proof that the data exist.
  - ○ Keep a log of the data restore tests.

Rules and Ramifications

☐ Negotiate the DR/COB plan with all stakeholders
- It is the responsibility of the project manager to insure that all aspects of the DR/COB plan are vetted and accepted by the stakeholders.
  - ○ The project council, the group composed of department heads or department representatives and other stakeholders, is an efficient venue to solidify agreement and approval.
  - ○ In the common case that some of the stakeholders disagree with a particular element of the plan, the least that the PM must obtain is an honest agreement to disagree at present while holding out the possibility of change in the future.
  - ○ Record, organize, and file issues for later reference.

☐ Document, **publish,** and make the plan readily available to all stakeholders in case of emergency.
- If a plan is not published and made available to the stakeholders, the plan is not finished.
  - ○ An unknown or unavailable plan is no plan at all.
  - ○ As mentioned before, beware of publishing or storing plans on media that require the very network and devices that may be impacted by a disaster.
  - ○ It is prudent to keep printed copies meant for technical team members and organization managers in various locations on-site and off-site.
  - ○ Insure that there is an element in your plan that mandates regular reviews and updates and republishes the disaster recovery plan.

☐ Review the plan in light of the "**law of unintended consequences.**"
- The law of unintended consequences offers wise advice to be cautious that you understand the potential consequences of and completely plan for all of the actions stipulated by the Project Plan. The exhaustive testing of all aspects of the DR/COB plans lessens the risk that the "law of unintended consequences" will appear.

☐ Do all elements of the plan adhere to the admonition within the Hippocratic Oath, "**First - do no harm**"?
- Hippocrates, author of the Hippocratic Oath taken by physicians, warns doctors to insure that well-intentioned actions to cure the patient do not instead harm them. Likewise, it is with DR/COB plans.
  - ○ As with the law of unintended consequences, diligent, incremental testing is the solution to potentially harmful plan elements.

Roles/Relegation/Responsibility/Reachable and Reactive

☐ Have appropriate people been assigned to specific roles and tasks?
- People given responsibility for any part of the project plan must be competent, willing, and otherwise able to exercise their responsibilities.
  - ○ Beware that senior managers do not assign their responsibility for the DR/COB plan to subordinates that are not qualified or not able to perform.
- Concerning the "ready, willing, and able" attributes needed for personnel assigned to DR/COB tasks, managers must consider health and family situations.
  - ○ For example, a single mother or father with young children may not be able to temporarily relocate to a remote DR/COB site.

☐ Who will be responsible to decide about and give the **declaration of emergency**?
- Senior management must decide the parameters of what constitutes a disaster, what level of disaster will be declared, and who will make the announcement.
  - ○ The importance of determining lines of authority cannot be overstated. If the parameters for phased disaster declarations and lines of authority are clouded, confusion and nonperformance will be the likely result.
  - ○ As with other critical elements of a DR/COB plan, these essential steps should be carefully designed, communicated, and periodically rehearsed.

☐ How will the emergency be communicated to various stakeholders?
- Exercise caution to insure that the announcement of the disaster is not blocked by the destruction of the communications modality you have chosen to use.
  - ○ **Have more than one communications methodology.** For example, if your plan calls for the declaration of emergency to be broadcast over the public address system and the electrical power has been cut, another way to contact organization members must be in place.
  - ○ One of the techniques to solve possible communications issues is to survey those individuals that have alternative phones, mobile communications devices like home phones, cell phones, pagers, and Blackberries. These devices should be included in the "alert pyramid" schema.
- An "**alert pyramid**" is a hierarchical list of personnel usually constructed from the top manager stepping down through subordinate groups to all relevant stakeholders.
  - ○ This pyramid contact methodology is very efficient as long as there is a feedback mechanism in place to indicate the contact success rate.
  - ○ If a level of the tree has been compromised with failure, alternate persons must fill in the breach and complete the alert pyramid.

○ Alert pyramid templates are included in chapter 5. Their testing and efficacy assessment is a mandatory part of any well-designed DR/COB plan.

☐ Do you know where your critical stakeholders are located?
- Similar to the contact methodology concerns stated above, the COB plan should consider all factors that might impede the ability to contact key or relevant personnel.
  ○ Beyond the various media solutions, including telephones, pagers, e-mail, and text messaging devices, a regularly updated plan should communicate timely information about where critical stakeholders will be located during vacations and off-site work.

☐ Will contacted personnel know where to go and what to do at the beginning and during a disaster?
- Do not wait until the last minute to select locations for critical personnel to gather.
  ○ Agree beforehand on places suitable to get together in the case of various disasters large, medium, and small.
  ○ When choosing potential locations, keep in mind that the people assembled will have basic human needs to satisfy.
  ○ More discussion about the requirements of alternative work sites will occur during future segments of this workbook.

Review/Revise/Rehearse/Refine/Retrain/Refrain Cycle

☐ Is the plan regularly reviewed and updated with periodic recurring revisions?

☐ Has the revised plan been rehearsed?

☐ Have the test result metrics been documented, collated, and interpreted for refinement of the plan with the addition of lessons learned?

☐ Have the disaster recovery participants been trained in light of ongoing revisions?

☐ Has the **project development life cycle** [PDLC] been periodically and realistically reframed in view of organizational expansion or contraction?

☐ Are metrics in place to allow a quantitative assessment of the efficacy of the plan?

☐ Go back to the beginning of the checklist!

The Importance of Testing—An Object Lesson

As an object lesson, the following real-life example reflects the necessity of testing the plan.

Several years ago, a part-time employee of the author announced that she had procured another part-time job. She had been hired to procure and install a tape backup unit in a small law firm. The tape backup was part of a simple DR/COB plan she devised that addressed the risk that the server hard drive might crash.

She related to me how she had set up an off-site tape rotation schedule and had trained one of the secretaries to remove the recorded tape and replace it with a new tape every morning. The recorded tape was duly stored at another office. Everything appeared to be in order to respond to a catastrophic server disk failure.

A few months later, she came into work looking very dejected. When asked about the reason for her melancholy, she responded that the attorneys had fired her and were about to file a lawsuit for damages against her.

It seemed that she had indeed implemented a DR/COB plan. She set up the tape unit, purchased the tapes, and created a backup plan. The secretary had dutifully rotated the tapes each day as instructed.

Therefore, when the server disk drive crashed, she purchased another hard disk drive. Onto it, she loaded and configured the operating system and commenced to restore the data that had been saved to the backup tape.

After several tries, she concluded with great consternation that the tapes did not have any data to restore. On investigation, it seems that the data cable from the tape drive connecting to the server had not been properly installed.

Her clients were badly hurt by the loss of their electronic data. Thousands of dollars had to be spent to re-construct the data stores from paper copies.

It was clear that if, as part of her simple COB plan, she had included an initial and periodic "restore from tape" test, the cable connection error would have been discovered and no harm would have been done.

The important lesson to learn from this true story is that real-world testing is an obligatory part of any DR/COB plan. If you have responsibility for a plan, you must constantly test all assumptions.

Readiness/Rapidity/Remoteness

☐ Have you created more than one DR/COB plan, prioritized based on the severity of the emergency, business need, or other criteria?

- Some organizations require multiple DR/COB plans. The building of multiple plans phased according to disaster severity can present a challenge but are necessary.
- The coordination of multiple disaster plans among various parts of an organization can be even more of a challenge. Be diligent and work through all permutations.
- Think of the execution of these plans as a ballet, not a blitzkrieg.
  - It is easy to write an aggressive plan with unrealistic assumptions and time lines. However, to achieve a workable plan, it is necessary to factor in all dependencies, including compensation for the foibles of human nature.
  - Understand and address potential problems caused by fear and other negative emotions during and after a disaster.

☐ Does the overall plan include a triage mechanism to decide which disaster plan or plan phase to invoke?
- Is there a triage process in place to determine "first things first," e.g., which are the most critical production functions that must be addressed first, second, etc.?
- Is there an informed and effective leader in charge?
  - Regardless of the written plan, there will be times where someone in charge must provide sensible leadership in view of a particular unusual situation.
- Does the triage process include decision criteria to decide if the execution of various emergency plans or phases of plans should be from local or remote locations?

☐ How much time to implementation is necessary to execute each phase of the recovery solution in the plan?
- The compilation and rehearsal of decision criteria that will engage a particular plan is as important as selecting a suitable individual or group to make the declaration of emergency and lead the plan.
  - If a group is necessary for decision-making, insure that there are alternates that can serve in the absence of one of the principals.
  - Insure that someone in the group has the authority to resolve disagreements.

☐ If the plan requires a remote site, is it far enough away to avoid the same disaster situation that affected the primary site?
- A rule of thumb that some organizations use regarding the minimum prudent distance for a remote site is no less than one hundred miles. If an organization is worried about weather system disasters, then it might wish to consider even greater distances away from the primary site.
  - However, keep in mind that many COB plans necessitate sending personnel from the primary site to the COB site.
    - Travel takes time.
    - Travel is expensive.
    - Travel disrupts employees' lives.

- Compare the safety of greater distance to the importance of a quicker recovery.

☐ Is the remote site kept at the ready?
- Is it equipped to provide the necessary capability for all levels of production recovery?
  - Have inventory lists been created of all necessary items to allow production work from the remote site?
  - Are the items checked against the inventory list on a regular basis?
- Are DR/COB tests actually conducted from the remote site to insure test integrity?

☐ How rapidly can workers be sent to the remote site?
- Has transportation been arranged to the remote site?
- Have room and board been arranged for the remote users?
- Have financial resources been budgeted to cover the expense of setting up and activating a remote capability?
  - Has disaster insurance been purchased to help defray the expense?

☐ Employee considerations
- Is there help for families with children or other dependents?
- Have employees with family obligations prepared for temporary relocation?
- Have arrangements been made to provide counseling services and assistance to the workers and families of workers that may have been traumatized or impacted deleteriously from the disaster?
- Is there an understanding between management and employees how hourly and salaried workers will be compensated in the case that they are required to be away from home for twenty-four hours, seven day a week?
  - Are there union rules to consider?
  - Has provision for additional wages been budgeted for DR/COB?

☐ If there is not a "**dark site**" (always-ready) remote site, can users access other organization resources via the Internet or other media?
- One alternative for remote DR/COB users is the "work from home" option. Given sufficient bandwidth and equipment, users can access a remote DR/COB site from home.
  - Implementing this option necessitates the installation of effective security mechanisms to secure the DR/COB site against improper intrusion from a remote source. In fact, the security schema at the DR/COB site should be no less than existed at the primary site.
- Another possibility for organizations owing multiple offices is the strategic relocation of certain critical personnel to noncritical company workstations in a different office facility.
  - This kind of plan requires the agreement and coordination of two facilities' management and technical teams at both sites to insure that it will be successful.

○ Keep in mind that relocating workers to the "go to" facility is disruptive. Plan to maintain production at the "go to" site.

☐ Include in your plan provision for up-to-date data resources at the alternate site.
- If the data stores have been destroyed at the primary site, how old are the offsite data backups?
- Can the business retain productivity from backup data that may be days old?
  ○ How new is necessary?
  ○ Has there been worst-case provision made for updating the backup to current levels using physical records?
  ○ Do not allow off-site data stores to age beyond usefulness.

Reversibility/Restoration/Recuperation/Resumption

- Can you efficiently **reverse** all disaster recovery actions in the case of false alarms or in the case of bona fide disasters that are quickly rectified?
- How does the primary computing and business environment get **restored** postdisaster?
  ○ Who will decide and announce the "all clear" when the emergency is over?
  ○ How will the "all clear" be communicated?
- Have you discussed with the stakeholders a hierarchy of events that must cascade to accomplish the organization's **recuperation** and **resumption** of business after the disaster has passed?
  ○ Are these events a part of your disaster plan?
- The DR/COB plan must address the **restoration** of the primary site with the **resumption** of business production.
  ○ Sometimes disaster plans mistakenly focus only on how the business maintains productivity at the remote DR/COB site.
  ○ Always ask the question and plan for, "What happens when the emergency is over"?
  ○ How does production move back to the primary site?
- Each emergency is different, so it is difficult to provide a complete business resumption checklist except to say that the restoration plan should likely look like a subset of the DR /COB migration plan, only in reverse.
- The concept of restoration is especially relevant to data stores.
  ○ **Different users must never simultaneously update (edit) copies of the same file at separate locations unless the updates are a part of a synchronized replication schema.**
  ○ If this happens, two different primary data sets then exist, and data integrity is lost.
  ○ The result of working from two primary data sets is a mess if, as is usual, it is not easy to recognize which records in a file have been added, deleted, or altered.

- In light of this dual data set problem, it is sometimes a good idea to use **thin clients** with a "client/server" or "client/host" architecture.
  - ○ If the business keeps the data in an accessible third location—for example, a "data center"—that offers WAN access for both the primary and remote locations, there will be only one data set to be updated, and no injury will need occur.
- **Beware!**
  - ○ Getting infrastructure and data restored at the primary site is every bit as complex as moving production to the remote site.
  - ○ Do not forget to plan for after the disaster.
- As you move users to the remote site, the data set used there may become the primary data set.
  - ○ Does the disaster plan arrange to back up the disaster site data set?
  - ○ It is a good idea to determine a time duration after which the secondary site will adapt the same robust disaster protections initially planned for the primary site.
- **To recap:**
  - ○ The reader should at this point conclude that disaster plans should be cyclical in nature.
  - ○ At any point along the continuum of doing business, you should ask the question "What if?"

Results / Deliverables

The following checklist of questions reiterates some of the things that should be accomplished by the end of the Design Phase of a disaster plan.

☐ Does the plan clearly define all major task, milestone and critical path items?

☐ Have time lines for expediting the tasks been determined?

☐ Do the stakeholders understand the consequence of not expediting critical path items?

☐ Do appropriate personnel have tasks assigned with expected delivery dates?

☐ Is the project manager tracking deliverables against the plan time line?

☐ Did the team complete a time and materials estimate?

☐ Has a plan "cost and benefits" estimate been compiled? (Include opportunity cost if appropriate.)

☐ Has an ROI presentation been prepared and presented to management?

☐ Have you defined how you are going to measure your results?
  • Did you commence the implementation of the metrics schema?

☐ Are the definitions of "success" vetted and confirmed by the stakeholders?
  • Make sure that senior management agrees with the goals.

☐ Has the DR/COB team taken a couple of steps back from the formal plan to conduct a brainstorming session to discover any overlooked, practical considerations that may provide either opportunities or problems during implementation?

☐ Have you planned for sufficient inventories of required equipment and other items necessary for the Implementation Phase?

☐ Do you have sufficient Implementation Phase staging space?

☐ Do you have sufficient qualified personnel?

☐ Have you identified and presented to management all production impact stipulations necessary for the implementation of the DR/COB plan?

☐ Has the project plan been iteratively tested, refined, and revised to insure the success of the implementation?

☐ Has the business requirements document's related cost estimates been recast to plus or minus 15% of the stipulated project end cost?

☐ Has the team finished the design document and prepared for a management presentation?

☐ Is there written management approval for the plan and a commitment of resources for implementation?

☐ Are dates fixed to implement the design?

☐ Have all cost and time estimates been adjusted to reflect contingencies?

☐ Are you prepared to follow the pattern: deploy, train, test, revise; deploy, train, test revise—ad infinitum?

☐ Do you use and publish the metrics schemas created to measure success and identify failure?

☐ Did you create and distribute a process control manual [PCM] that stipulates the standard operating procedures [SOP] for maintenance of the plan?

☐ Are you meeting periodically with stakeholders and the project council to pass along advice, consent, updates, and information?

Summary of Chapter 3

The concepts contained in chapter 3 form the conceptual core of this workbook. The "Cluster of *Rs*" will allow the reader to grasp many important concerns involved when designing and deploying a DR/COB plan.

The question that connects all of the items in chapter 3 is "What if?" If project managers can continually ask "What if?" the answers will help build a successful DR/COB plan.

The other major concept in this chapter is the discovery and remediation of "single points of failure." A robust system must have redundancy.

CHAPTER 4

LESSONS LEARNED—OPINION AND ADVICE

Ethics

■ Do not overlook the application of ethical principles to all aspects of project management.

■ Some rules to follow:
   ☐ Do not accept any special favors from those you have engaged to provide or are in the process of deciding to provide service or equipment for the project.
   ☐ While the meaning of "favors" may not include a cheap pen or a coffee cup, it may include paying for lunch, dinner, sports tickets, trips, or discounts on equipment.
   ☐ Very few in for-profit business give anything to anyone without expectations. Do not allow your integrity to be "bought" for the price of a lunch. If you need to go to lunch with a vendor, pick up or split the check.
   ☐ If you are a manager, treat all subordinates in a correct and consistent manner.
   ☐ Don't be a bully!
   ☐ The best managers view themselves as a resource for their subordinates.
   ☐ If you delegate responsibility, do not insist on unreasonable results that are constrained by either resources or authority.
   ☐ Do not be bullied by superiors to agree with approaches that are, in your estimate, potentially failure prone or unethical. In a respectful manner, stipulate your view of possible deleterious consequences of activities with which you disagree.

Project Approach

The following items represent helpful ideas and conclusions derived from many years of project management experience.

☐ **Organization**

Approach the planning of DR/COB in a serious and deliberate manner within a classic project management paradigm. This kind of approach is important for success, as it promotes a logical organization of goals from the start to the end of the project.

☐ **Cooperation and Communication**

To insure success, predicate the implementation of a successful DR/COB project on close cooperation and effective communication between the organization (business), the technology team, and other stakeholders.
- Most managers who have helped to bring DR/COB plans to fruition understand the importance of this lesson.

☐ **Wishful Thinking**

Sometimes people write an unworkable COB plan simply to have a plan.
- These same people do not test their assumptions but indulge in "wishful thinking," hoping or assuming that the plan will work.
- When managing risk using a disaster plan, "wishful thinking" is sometimes more dangerous than having no plan at all.
  - If the organization is depending on a dysfunctional plan, it may be lulled into a false sense of well-being.
  - If disaster does then strike, the shock of DR/COB plan failure simply adds to the confusion and inability to recover in a deliberate and timely manner.

☐ **Unnecessary Complexity and Cost**

In-house technical teams or vendors sometimes recommend excessively complex and expensive DR/COB solutions when a simpler plan would suffice.
- Judgments must be carefully made to insure that the target of the plan is worthy of saving in light of the cost to save it.
- Both sides of the "cost/benefits" equation must be in balance to insure that there is a potential benefit return on DR/COB investment.

☐ **Life Cycle Paradigm**

All processes and projects, including complex DR/COB projects, should have a beginning, a middle, and an end.

- The end of the project should segue into another project's beginning to include necessary revisions.
- This cyclical project characteristic explains why classic project management is often referred to as a "life cycle" plan. One plan life ends and another begins.
- The cycle of designing, implementing, testing, and revising allows for constant plan improvement.

☐ Overlapping Project Phases

Phases of a project plan as described in this book often overlap in their functionality.
- While the project itself is a continuum, the phases point to virtual beginnings and endings.
- While there is indeed overlap between the phases, you will find them useful to reference and help track progress.

☐ Plan

Plan your course of action in a deliberate and professional manner. Do not act capriciously or casually.
- Engage the organization.
- Discover the plan.
- Design the plan.
- Work the plan.
- Test the plan.
- Close the plan.
- Maintain the plan.

☐ Expect Change and Prepare to Deal with It

"Nothing is constant except change itself" is a paraphrase of a wise aphorism first attributed to the Greek philosophers Heraclitus and then Plato.
- A corollary: Keep cool and placid in the understanding that the unexpected always happens. Accept that changes to some part of your plan will always be necessary.
- While inconvenient, changes can also serve as an opportunity to make your plan more effective.
- Said one more time:
  - Insure that the understanding with the project sponsor (management), whether written or verbal, includes the ability to obtain more resources (time/money) if the scope of the project should change.

☐ **Opportunities for Creative Solutions during Crisis**

View inharmonic moments when things appear to go wrong as an opportunity for positive and creative solutions.

- Consider team progress retreats and regrouping as steps toward a renewed start, increased efficiency, and a successful conclusion.
- If the business requirements change, then your DR and COB plan should change as well.
- Make sure to update and publish all copies of the plan simultaneously.

☐ **Cushion the Negative Impact of Surprises**

If you carefully analyze ongoing progress and aggressively seek reasons to revise your plan to make it more efficient, surprise glitches are less likely to find you unprepared and disadvantaged.

- Remember to explore mistakes with the entire team.
- Never single out an individual for negative criticism in public.
  - ○ Correct negative behaviors of team members in private.
- Do not gossip about criticism or corrective actions. Keep them confidential.
- Seek collective solutions to issues instead of assigning individual blame.
- If appropriate, clarify team member responsibilities during a group meeting.
- Ask for feedback to gather "lessons learned" data.

☐ **Authority to Proceed**

Pre-engagement activity is critical. To be successful, you must possess the appropriate authority to discharge your responsibilities.

- If the authority is not already sufficient in your present organizational level or position in the client business, then an appropriate sponsor must delegate it to you.
- Ignore this rule at your own risk.

☐ **Scope Creep**

Resist accepting responsibility for add-on tasks that you do not have the specific authority and resources to discharge successfully within the plan.

- The danger of unplanned project expansion is sometimes called "scope creep."
- "Scope creep" is often unintentionally insidious. It can sneak up on a team that accepts small, incremental changes to the project plan without proper discovery and design analysis.
- Accept project scope changes, both additions and subtractions, only after planning and always with a written addendum to the original plan
  - ○ Do not forget to ask for increased resources if necessary.

☐ **Task List Compilation**

During the Pre-engagement Phase or, at the latest, the Engagement Phase, you must start to compose a list of tasks, understand why the tasks need to be accomplished and in what order and time frame they must be accomplished, and have at least a general sense of how to proceed.

- One of the very important elements of task compilation is the creation of a hierarchical list that stipulates primary and subordinate tasks.
- Identify milestones and critical path task items.
- A milestone represents the completion of a top-level, important task.
- A critical path item is a task that, if not completed within the stipulated time frame, will affect the timely completion of the overall project.

☐ **Define Success Up Front**

Negotiate goals with the sponsor. Deal with unambiguous, specific outcomes within an allotted budget and time frame that will be viewed as "success."

- If these agreed-upon goals are not clear, the project may meander, and your best efforts may ultimately be viewed as short of the mark.
- Write the list of goals against a time line and budget, and get acceptance by all interested parties (stakeholders).

☐ **Verbal Agreement Amnesia**

If you fail to get explicit written confirmation of the metrics that define success, you may encounter mysterious amnesia from otherwise mentally healthy organizational sponsors from whom you had only verbal agreements.

- In the slang of an old management mentor, "If it ain't written, it ain't!"
- Business management forgetfulness may be unintentional. Persons in top management are usually very busy, and your project may not be on the peak of their list of concerns.

☐ **Additional Work Usually Means Additional Resources**

Said again, if a project sponsor wants to alter the DR/COB business requirements goals list (scope creep), make sure that person understands that the addition may require additional resources.

- Avoid this topic at your peril.
- Define the problem of "scope creep" prior to your signoff of the business requirements document.
- Stipulate a process to negotiate any expansion of the project.

☐ **Know the "Players"**

In your tenure as a project manager, you may hear the term "player" in reference to an individual. The term "player" in a business organization is someone who is a decision maker, can influence a decision maker, or in some other way be instrumental in moving the project forward.

- A player within a client organization may be a management person.
- A player on a project team is a knowledge expert, creative critic, problem solver and/or decision maker.

- The project manager must know the players and their hot buttons.
  - Hot buttons are specific issues or items that elicit a knowledgeable response.
  - Nurture the players.
  - Know them on a first-name basis if possible.

□ **Guard against Project Team Malcontents and Incompetents**

Try your best to move away quickly from "dysfunctional people" on your team.

- If someone on the team is hostile, negative, passive aggressive, or incompetent to the extent that he or she is an impediment to progress, get him or her away from the team as quickly as possible.
- The danger to the team increases as serious complainers try to validate their negative issues. They will often interact and solicit co-workers to their cause in an attempt to foment dissention.
- Do not be paranoid, but do be prudent in exercising your responsibility as a manager to maintain team morale.
- A good manager will act in a proactive manner to counsel against negative behaviors.
- A good manager will also provide many opportunities for team members to approach him with concerns.
  - Good managers listen attentively and respond seriously to expressions of concern.
- Always understand the host organization's policy regarding employment issues.
  - Consult with a Human Resources person before taking any prejudicial action against a team member.
  - If the team member is a temporary employee, consult with the firm that employs him.

□ **Organize Efficient, Effective Meetings**

In the very early stages of the project, decide when, where, and how to conduct meetings.

- Solicit information about times that might be most convenient for most of the stakeholders.
  - Because managers are busy, expect that this task will be difficult.
  - Rely on your understanding of the "pecking" order and accommodate decision makers first.
- Publish an agenda with an approximate time given to address each listed issue.
- If items need specific expert input, alert responsible persons in time for them to come to the meeting prepared.
- After the group addresses specific agenda items, always ask if there are questions before moving on.
  - Leave time for questions at the end of the meeting.

- A good meeting has a planned beginning, middle, and end. Stick to your agenda and your schedule. You will invite disinterest or even derision if you do not respect team members' time.
- Curtail digressions that are off the agenda. When identified, if the topic is worthy, set aside for the agenda of a future meeting.
- As a rule, in a meeting, the best project managers listen 60% and talk 40% or less.
- You will discover that "leading" or "open-ended" questions are much more productive than statements.
- An interrogative or conditional approach to reaching team decisions or consensus is most effective.
    - For example, ask:
        - What does the group think about…?
        - Does the team prefer…?
        - Should we decide to …?
        - Are there any objections to…?
- Write down or have someone else write the minutes of the meeting.
    - Distribute the meeting minutes soon after the meeting and again just prior to the next meeting.
- To promote the critical reading of the published minutes, ask for a comment on an item in the minutes.
    - Keep track of the responses and gently confront the nonresponders.

☐ **Take Charge**

As a project manager, you must take charge of the agenda and tend to the project plan.
- It is your responsibility to plan the meetings, author the reports, procure the resources, and lead the team to complete the project!
- Demonstrably taking charge is a key concept that will allow a leader to exercise a greater degree of control over outcomes.
- Taking charge does not mean acting as a tyrant.
    - Taking charge does mean aggressively seeking consensus from the group.

☐ **Delegate Responsibility Only with the Appropriate Resources**

One more time: If you delegate control to a subordinate, insure that sufficient resources are available and authority given to insure success.
- There is nothing as pitiful as the assignment of responsibility for a task or project without granting the requisite authority and resources to take control and get it done.

☐ **Communication is Paramount to Success**

The more time you spend on developing, defining, and refining business requirements and rehearsing goals, ways, and means with senior managers and team members, the less unpleasant time you will have to spend justifying why there was a delay.

- Take seriously management's potential for a negative perception of a nondelivery or a late delivery.
- The solution for misunderstandings is constant and quality communication.

☐ Questions Are as Important as Answers

Right answers are difficult—even more so is asking the right questions.

- A third-level novice can research an answer to a well-stipulated question or issue.
- Work on honing your skill as an interviewer.
  - ○ Be prepared before you sit down with an interviewee.
  - ○ Ask interviewees what questions you should ask them.
- A good project manager knows how to work interrogatively with management and users to evoke a precise, comprehensive business requirements document, within which are clearly defined expectations and goals, including general means to a successful end.

☐ Homework

Do the necessary homework to be familiar with the project prior to starting.

- It is the PM's responsibility to know most of the questions to ask at all levels of the project.
- You cannot ask the right questions if you do not have an in-depth understanding of the nature of the client organization.
  - ○ The same is true for an understanding of the tools and processes used to create a DR/COB plan.

☐ Write It Down

Everything worthy to be remembered should be written down.

- Do not trust your memory.
- Write all of it down in a retrievable place and format.
- Review your notes regularly!
- Using an electronic, keyword-searchable text editor is an efficient way to find previous project content.
- Write and keep copious notes about times, people, places, meetings, etc.
- Written records can avoid missed deadlines and misconceptions due to lapses of memory or hidden agendas.
- Well-organized, written records also provide a good way to track the history of a project.
- Records lend to the creation of "lessons learned." A review of these lessons allows for subsequent performance improvement.

☐ Use Electronic Mail

Communicate important inquiries and commitments by e-mail instead of the telephone.
- If you do (and you certainly will) have verbal conversations, send memorandums of understanding confirming those conversations.

☐ Be Aware of the Organizational Pecking Order

Understand who in the organization reports to whom. You want to know, as soon as possible, who has the power to make decisions.
- If at all possible or relevant, you may want to orient your attention to any political pecking-order issues first.
  - Who are the more influential and who are less influential managers?
- If the senior manager is satisfied with your performance and is a project advocate, this person may protect you from those subordinates in the organization that might have some reason to see you fail.

☐ Understanding Organizational Politics is Important for Success

As an addition to the pecking order concerns, be aware that some project tasks often take precedence because of organizational politics.
- Relax and deal with it gracefully.
- Be positive in your demeanor, but define any negative implications of the delay for management.

☐ Prioritize

Many technical tasks necessitate prioritized dependencies because of the availability of resources.
- A project manager should arrange tasks carefully in view of task dependencies.
  - A dependent task is one that must wait for the preceding task to be completed.
- It will help if you keep in mind that tasks do not necessarily have to occur one after another but may be done in parallel to achieve greater efficiency.

☐ Do Not Speculate

Do not speculate about enhanced project possibilities, including casual claims of enhanced capabilities.
- Loose lips sink schemas!
- For example, facing an extemporaneous request from management, you may be unwise to immediately respond, "Not a problem—we can do that." Rather, say, "Let us look into that and I'll get back to you."
  - Do look into it.
  - Do get back on a timely basis.

  ○ Do recalculate the cost of the revised business requirement document, project
    scope, and time line.

☐ **Stand Your Ground**

There may be times when you or your team must save the customer organization from itself!
- Do not get intimidated by anyone into making commitments that are not feasible, prudent, or legal.
- Regardless of how exalted the author of an "out-of-plan" or unfeasible request, it is likely that you alone will own the initiative if the outcome does not meet expectations.

☐ **Guard Against Overly Aggressive Time Lines and Budgets**

Do not be a hero! If the project will strain to be finished comfortably in a month, plan for a little more than a month.
- Do not be hurried beyond your capability to deliver.
  ○ Always leave a little margin for error.
- In like manner, be reasonably generous with your estimates of cost.
  ○ It is easier to return excess money to the organization and be a viewed as competent rather than to appear hapless if you must ask for more resources due to an insufficient budget.
- Of course, be frugal with resources, efficient in the conduct of your activities, and ruthless in rooting out waste in project work.

☐ **Keep Meticulous Records of Expenses**

Among all of the dilemmas that a project manager can find himself in is the inability to justify or explain the project expenditures.
- If you do not have the expertise to do project financial accounting, add an accountant to your staff. For large projects, accountants are an expense that most senior managers are willing to meet.

☐ **Sometimes It Is Better to Ask for Forgiveness than Permission**

If necessary, it is sometimes better to ask for forgiveness than for permission. This is a wonderful rule taught to the author by a project manager mentor.
- During an emergency, multilayered permissions can delay a solution and even exacerbate a situation.
- Do not attempt to hide these "time is of the essence" decisions. Announce them as though you are in charge.
- Of course, do not be reckless or arrogant.
- Of course, do be reasonable and right.

☐ **Presenting Information for Best Understanding**

Tailor your presentation vocabulary to your audience.

- You should not communicate to most business management groups in esoteric technical terms or acronyms.
- For reasons of bonding, you may define and teach a couple of esoteric technical terms that your client can pass knowingly up the line to equally nontechnical managers.
- While the use of acronyms and technical terms can be counterproductive in a general business forum, do not dumb down general vocabulary or use improper grammar—spoken or written.
- Generally, people show enhanced respect for others that have a good command of their presentation language.
- Do not assume that nontechnical users or managers have any understanding of technical issues.
- Likewise, do not assume that they do not have any understanding of technical issues.
- Before a presentation, try to determine the technical level of your audience. If the assembly has mixed expertise, speak to the lowest common denominator.
- Given a nontechnical audience, your presentations will likely be successful if you stay focused on project features, benefits, and especially return on investment.
- The use of visual presentations and simple, high-level explanations are often enough to get understanding and a nod of agreement.

☐ Speak Not of Cost, but Investment

You must speak clearly to senior management about project time lines, production impact to the organization, and investment return.

- Do not characterize funding as "cost" or "expense," but use the term "investment."
  - ○ Investments should always expect a monetary return.
- Be prepared to explain how the project will have a return on investment [ROI]. Business managers usually respond positively to a good return on investment presentation.
  - ○ When you build your project budget, include ROI.
- If attending managers' eyes gloss over during a project presentation, talking about ROI can sometimes retrieve their attention.
- Keep discussions focused around solutions to requirements, e.g., features and benefits.
- Be prepared to explain "opportunity cost" for those project initiatives that may be rejected.
  - ○ Opportunity cost or opportunity loss is, said another way: What is the cost or potential loss for not doing a particular thing?

☐ DR/COB Project—Impact to Production

Do not ignore the potential negative impact of your DR/COB project on daily business production.

- Be prepared to negotiate with management some ways to decrease the impact of interruptions to daily routines.

☐ Don't Be Hoodwinked by Vendors

Beware of vendors bearing magical solutions or tickets to the World Series, and cast a wary eye on remarkable product claims.
- Keep in mind that all salespersons want to make or maintain a sale. While there is certainly nothing wrong with wanting to make a sale, make sure to check references and compare solutions and prices.
- You should treat vendors fairly but at arm's length and with circumspection.
- Use vendors to teach you solutions.
- Purchase the best deal for the organization you represent.
- Act in an honest, forthright, and ethical manner at all times.

☐ Be a Team Resource, Not an "Ivory Tower" Boss

The most successful project managers serve less as a boss than as a resource to and a leader for their team. In a sense, they work for their subordinates to insure the team's success.
- Spend a portion of your day interacting with your team and, if possible, actually help with some of their tasks.

☐ To Get Respect, Give Respect

Directed anger, exasperation, disrespect, disregard, or condescension toward subordinates has no place in good project management.
- When things go wrong, lower your voice while seeking solutions
- What you give to team members is usually what you will receive from them. Respect begets respect.

☐ The Law of Inertia

Sometimes the project manager must fight against what is analogous to Newton's First Law of Inertia. To wit: organizations at rest tend to stay still without an outside impetus. In the context of disaster recovery, this principal suggests that outdated technologies and processes tend to become increasingly comfortable and intractable over time. Process familiarity often causes progress and positive change to stall.
- The learning of new technologies or processes always carries some psychological pain for end users. Good communications and training are the solutions for making discomforted users feel better about new technology.
- Do not forget to include training in your project plan.
- Emphasize the importance of training for the plan's success.
- Include training expense in your budget.

☐ Team-building

Team-building and leadership techniques are very important to a successful project manager. This importance stems from the enhanced efficacy and efficiency of harmonious teams. Member harmony and enthusiasm for project excellence are team attributes that make a tremendously positive impact on outcomes. However, it is beyond the scope of this text to go into depth about the many different team-building methodologies.

- I recommend that any new project manager not already familiar with team-building and leadership skills research the literature available concerning these techniques. Some of the research and documented "best practice" done over the years can be very helpful in understanding team dynamics.
  - For example, one can enhance understanding of team dynamics by reading about Tuckman's organizational team-building stages of "forming, storming, norming, and performing"[6] that invariably attend a new team or a system change in an organization.
  - It has been my experience that both the user community and the technical crew exemplify these Tuckman stages until they become acclimated to a new way of doing things.

Summary of Chapter 4

Without a well-organized and tested DR/COB plan coordinated with the responsible information technology group, an organization can be negatively impacted by a disaster that interrupts their production.

A plan to decrease the negative effect of an emergency is not an expense—it is an investment.

If a production process is valuable to an organization, a plan to decrease the negative effect of an emergency is not an expense—it is an investment in the survival of the business.

As is advocated by this book, using a classic project management paradigm as an approach to accomplish all disaster recovery and continuity of business plans is highly recommended. The same advice holds true for all major business and information technology projects.

---

6.   B. W. Tuckman, "Developmental sequences in small groups," Psychological Bulletin 63 (1965), 384-399.

CHAPTER 5

FORMS AND CHECKLISTS

Redundancy/Replication Checklist

A single point of system failure is counter to good disaster planning. The following are some of the things you should consider.

o Not all of these checklist items and recommendations are suitable for all situations.

o The size of the business and the criticality of the business process are important factors to consider when considering the relevance of the following checklist.

o Always be mindful that the cost of a solution must be measured against the cost of production failure.

☐ Critical spare parts have been indentified and are on hand or available in sufficient quantities to quickly fix existing primary site LAN attached equipment in place.

☐ You have identified more than one vendor to provide complex repairs, equipment replacement, expertise, and temporary staffing.

☐ Vendor contact information is included in your completed and published PCM (process control manual).

☐ Extra workstations, including monitors, have been set aside, set up, and maintained in an alternate location to accommodate COB activity in case of disaster.

☐ LAN copper and fiber runs to wiring closets and between wiring closets and the server/communication room are sufficiently redundant to reroute data packets should one of the circuits be severed.

☐ Physically wired "tech plates" routed to wiring closet patch panels should have at least four ports to allow for multiple workstation devices and insure repatching flexibility.

☐ Populate switches and/or hubs and routers with spare ports and subnet IP addresses in excess of the number needed for current user connectivity.
- ○ The extra switch cards and addressed ports are necessary in case one of the switch or hub cards fails.
- ○ Some organizations hosting critical data also store a standby switch chassis.

☐ If your LAN switch ports are managed from a remote or centralized location (a common circumstance in large organizations), insure that there is an emergency modality that will allow quick reserve port activation.

☐ Switches and/or hubs and routers are redundant and "crosshatched" with failover capability.
- • It is rare but possible that an entire switch/hub/router can fail.
- • It is more common that a port card installed in the switch/hub/router can fail.
- • Crosshatching of patch cables between two or more port cards, switches or hubs can insure that should one of the devices fail only a percentage of user connections will be lost during the time it takes to install a replacement.
  - ○ For example, only 50% of user connections are at risk if two switches are crosshatched—four switches = 25%, etc.

☐ All WAN circuits are redundant and crosshatched.
- • Long-distance circuits have three parts:
  - ○ The local loop from the site to the telephone company [CO]
  - ○ The long haul carrier
  - ○ The local loop at the terminus of the circuit
- • Crosshatch redundant local loop telephony vendors with redundant long haul carriers.
  - ○ This schema insures that the failure of any one vendor, local or long haul carrier, does not put WAN connectivity at risk.

☐ If the organization uses a private branch exchange [PBX] for voice telephony, does the site have nonswitched trunk lines to the CO [telephone company] to get access to the outside world if the PBX [private branch exchange or on-site phone switch] fails?
- • An off PBX switch, plain old telephone line [POT] phone should be in every "tech room" to insure communication to the outside world in case of complete power failure.

☐ Is emergency lighting available in the case of power failure?
- • Are working flashlights available? Are extra batteries available?

☐ Are "stand-alone" mobile communication devices like walkie-talkies or cell phones available?

☐ Insure that redundant telephony circuits have different points of entry into the facility.

- Check to see if all of the circuits are coming from the same telephone pole. If they are all attached to the same pole, have the telephone company disperse them.

☐ In similar manner, insure that electrical power lines have different points of entry into the facility.
- Check to see if they have diverse source locations outside of the facility.
- If two public power grids are not available for diversity of supply, consider the installation of an electric generator of sufficient power output and operational duration to keep at least the critical equipment operating.

☐ Power cables to the tech rooms should have redundant feeds.
- A sufficiently responsive uninterrupted power supply [UPS] system should stand between the equipment and the outside power source.
  - The UPS should provide sufficient time after power failure for the electrical generator to switch on or for the technical staff to alert the user base and shut down sensitive equipment in an orderly manner.

☐ Does an electrical generator(s) stand ready to supply power to the system should "street power" fail?
- Generators need fuel to operate.
- Decide how much fuel needs to be stored to last for a sufficient number of hours or days.
- Know more than one vendor to call for a fuel delivery should you need more.

☐ If your power is gone during an emergency, other electric power users in your area are likely to be similarly affected.
- Understand that fuel vendors will be very busy, order the fuel with sufficient lead-time for delivery.
- Maintain sufficient generator fuel reserves for at least two days of operation.
- Because fuel vendors usually service their existing customer base first, forward-looking contracts are a good idea.

☐ After the power outage is over, continue with the generator power for at least a couple of hours.
- Street power sometimes fails again soon after recovery.

☐ When you finally do switch back to street power and the emergency is over, immediately top off your electric generator fuel tank in preparation for the next emergency.

☐ You have performed data backup/replication in a manner that allows quick restoration of either individual files or entire data servers.
- Negotiate data restoration timeliness with the business organization in accordance with their DR/COB needs.

- Insure that the organization understands data restoration time lines. The information should be in the PCM (process control manual).

☐ Cross train IT staff in different LAN management functions to create redundant functional LAN maintenance capability.
- During an emergency, if a key technician is incapacitated or absent, another staff member should be able to immediately pick up his or her functions.

☐ Has the business organization adapted a similar redundant personnel function policy for its production processes?

☐ Does the organization have redundant "proof of application license" or license keys stored off site to insure its availability should primary site platforms be destroyed and rebuilds become necessary?

☐ Are redundant network user profiles stored off site to insure their availability should primary site platforms be destroyed and rebuilds necessary?
- Are network user profiles regularly updated?
- Are server and desktop builds "ghosted" [replicated] for quick restore?

☐ Finally, yet importantly, have you tested your assumptions to insure that they will actually work?

Level Three Cost Estimate - Sample Form

It is common for management to require three estimates or cost ranges. The first level (+/- 50%) is prepared during the Engagement Phase. The second level (+/-25%) is prepared after the Discovery Phase, and the third (+/-5%) after the Design Phase. Because these dollar amounts are budgeted, it is important that the project manager does not exceed the amounts planned.

LEVEL THREE COST ESTIMATE

Level Three Divergence From Final Expense Allowed %:

Project Name:
Project ID:
Project Manager:
Team Lead:
Engineer:

```
┌─────────────────────────────────┐
│ Engineer:                       │
├─────────────────────────────────┤
│ Cost Code:                      │
└─────────────────────────────────┘
```

Project Staffing Expense:

Estimated Full-Time Equivalents   # FTEs: Total FTE Cost:

Per-Hour Cost:

Total Project Staffing Cost US$:

Description	Quantity	Item Cost	Other Cost	Total Cost
Hardware Expense:				
Workstations				
Server				
PDS				
Hubs				
Switches				
Router				
Power Circuits				
Data Circuits				
Other				
Total Hardware Cost US$:				
Software Expense:				
Total Software Cost US$:				
Other Vendor Expense				
Total Other Vendor Cost US$:				
One-Time Expenses				
Total One-time Cost US$:				
Ongoing Expense (Maintenance)				
Total Ongoing Cost US$:				

Financial Impact of Failure—BASIC Form

You can expand this basic spreadsheet to include more processes and financial impact factors. The intent of the exercise is to calculate the cost of not having an effective COB plan in force. Use the results to support opportunity cost and return on investment arguments for plans of different scope and expense.

Process	Annual Process Revenue	Est.# of Days Impact	Net Est. Revenue Impact (#Days X Daily Revenue)	Est. Extra Expenses	#of Replacement Staff	Expenses for Replacement Staff	Est. Total Financial Impact

Meeting Agenda With Last Meeting Minutes— Sample Form

Stipulating a plan to expedite meetings is a hallmark of a good project manager. A well-composed agenda adds discipline and efficiency to meetings. The sample meeting agenda template below can be expanded as needed.

TODAY'S DATE: XXXXXX

Meeting	<Name of Project>				
Local Meeting Place? Where?					
Day:		Date:		Time:	
Domestic Call-in #:		Int'l Call-in #:		PIN:	

<u>Meeting Facilitator/Leader:</u>

Name:

<u>Meeting Scribe/Minutes Taker:</u>

Name:

<u>Expected Participants:</u>

      I.   .

      2.   .

<u>Attendance: Role Call</u>

      I.   .

      2.   .

<u>Last Meeting Minutes</u>
Attach last meeting minutes document.

This meeting agenda items:

Agenda item:	*<Description>*
Item Assigned To	*<Person responsible for deliverable>*
Comments/Status	*<Task notes>*
Preparation/Dependencies	
Desired Outcome	
Meeting Time Allocated	
Follow-up Tasks	
Task Due By	

Copy agenda items outline as needed.

Disaster Alert Contact Pyramid Test Guidelines

An alert contact pyramid is a collection of DR/COB plan participants organized in a hierarchical fashion by department and/or function for the purpose of efficient contact and interaction in an emergency.

- The person at the top of a section of the tree contacts the individuals below him or her on the list using one of several communications modalities.
- When the contact list calling is completed, the lower-level persons report contact success or failure back up through the organizational tree to the coordinator at the top.
- When testing this system, keep metrics to assess functionality and insure that all contact information is current.
- For contacting stakeholders in the case of a disaster, provide the instructions and guidelines below to all parties responsible for making telephone calls.

Instructions:

1. Get the current employee call list report and distribute the document to all parties responsible for making telephone calls.
2. The individuals responsible for making calls will complete their calling section by indicating the date and time in the column provided.
3. The individuals responsible for making calls will also assess appropriate numeric scores measuring the call parameters. These numbers will be used to determine the alert pyramid grade and create an "alert contact pyramid efficiency metric."
4. The coordinator will collect all of the information from the parties responsible for making calls, and will complete the alert pyramid test summary sheet.

5. Forward only the alert pyramid test summary sheet to your DR/COB coordinator (see the bottom of the memo for names and fax numbers, and retain the supporting documents in accordance with the records retention policy of the particular organization.)

Additional Guidelines:

1. When a top manager speaks to a subordinate manager, she should verbally verify the contact names and numbers for that section of the alert pyramid with the subordinate manager.
2. Conduct the test after normal business hours to ensure that you can reach staff at their residences.
   a.   Do not schedule the test with staff in advance.
   b.   Surprise alert pyramids provide realistic results.
3. Be reasonable when selecting the time to conduct your alert pyramid.

Alert Pyramid—Contact Sheet Sample Form

Department Name: _____

Primary Caller: _____

Date of Test: _____   If Retest, Date of Original Test: _____

Contact Name (primary)	Contact Name
Work#	Work#
Home#	Home#
Cell#	Cell#
E-mail	E-mail
Date and time of contact: Score:	Date and time of contact: Score:
Contact Name	Contact Name
Work#	Work#
Home#	Home#
Cell#	Cell#
E-mail	E-mail
Date and time of contact: Score:	Date and time of contact: Score:
Contact Name	Contact Name
Work#	Work#
Home#	Home#
Cell#	Cell#
E-mail	E-mail
Date and time of contact: Score:	Date and time of contact: Score:
Contact Name	Contact Name
Work#	Work#
Home#	Home#
Cell#	Cell#
E-mail	E-mail
Date and time of contact: Score:	Date and time of contact: Score:

Number of Contacts to Call   _____

Number Contacted   _____

Percentage Successful   _____

Indicate Date of Re-test for Departments with $< 75\%$ _____

Manager: _____

Date: _____

Alert Pyramid Contact Test Metrics Worksheet

Collect points on your completed employee call list report based on the following point system:

Result Description	Points
Success: Person reached, returned message or page	I
Partial: Message left on machine or with family member, and call back to coordinator is made but not in a timely manner:	½
Failure: Unable to reach or leave message. Incorrect number on file	0

<u>Calculate your grade</u>:

Enter the sum of the points collected from the employee
call list report: _____

Divide the sum or the points by the number of calls made
and multiply by 100 to determine your rating percentage: _____

If your results are less than 75%, the test was unsatisfactory, and a retest is required within 30 days.

<u>Mediating factors</u>:

What was the total number of employees not contacted because they were on disability or on vacation?_____

Other mediating factors:

DR/COB Remote Site Planning Form

This detailed multipart planning form is one of several checklists in this workbook to assist in the discovery process when planning for a remote DR/COB site. Use it in conjunction with other forms and checklists in chapter 5. Feel free to add or subtract whatever material is appropriate for your situation.

Target Organization Information Form

Unit Name: _____ COB ID: _____

Provide a brief description of this business unit:

Indicate the management reporting structure of the target business unit up to the level of division head. Attach an organizational chart, or draw one below.

Business Locations Form

Indicate where the target business unit is located:

Primary Building Location
Address: _____
City: _____ State: _____ Zip: _____
Number of employees at this location: _____

Secondary Building Location (if applicable)
Address: _____
City: _____ State: _____ Zip: _____
Number of employees at this location: _____

Tertiary Building(s) Location (if applicable)
Address: _____
City: _____ State: _____ Zip: _____
Number of employees at this location: _____

- Are there additional building locations?
  If yes, attach a separate document showing all location addresses and number of employees.

Business Managers Information Form

The facility business manager will be responsible for all deliverable sign-offs within the department / business unit. If more than one, add appropriate information by copying and pasting the template that follows.

Name: _____ Title: _____
Building Location: _ Primary _ Secondary _ Tertiary _ Other
Office Phone: _____   E-mail: _____
Fax Number: _____   Mobile Phone: _____
Pager Number: _____   Home Phone: _____

COB/DR Coordinators Form

The COB/DR coordinator will be responsible for coordinating all deliverables for the department/business unit. Keep in mind that in large organizations, the DR information technology (IT) coordinator and the COB (business) coordinator may be different people. If they are different people supporting different emergency sites, please add appropriate differential information. Copy and paste to replicate the template that follows.

COB___   DR__
Name: _____ Title: _____
Building Location: _ Primary _ Secondary _ Tertiary _ Other
Office Phone: _____ E-mail: _____
Fax Number: _____ Mobile Phone: _____
Pager Number: _____ Home Phone: _____

COB/DR Coordinator Alternates Form

The COB/DR Coordinator Alternate will be responsible for coordinating all deliverables for the department/business unit in the event that the COB/DR coordinator is not available.
COB___   DR__
Name: _____ Title: _____
Building Location: _ Primary _ Secondary _ Tertiary _ Other
Office Phone: _____ E-mail: _____
Fax Number: _____ Mobile Phone: _____
Pager Number: _____ Home Phone: _____

Existing COB/DR Recovery Site Locations Form

Indicate where your existing recovery site(s) are:
COB:

- Not applicable or does not exist
- Mobile or at home
- Dedicated independent site
- Is the site functional and ready to go? Yes No
- Site shared with same business at another location (parallel processing)

Primary Site Address: _____
Tertiary Recovery Address: _____

DR:

- Not applicable or does not exist
- Mobile or at home
- Dedicated independent site
- Is the site functional and ready to go? Yes No
- Site shared with same business other location

Primary Site Address: _____

Tertiary Recovery Address: _____

How many business users will be assigned to each site? _____

How many technicians will be assigned to each site? _____

COB/DR Distance Matrix Form

Complete the following distance matrix, showing the distance (in miles) between the business location(s) and the recovery site location(s):

	Primary Business Location	Secondary Business Location	Other Business Location
DR *Site* Location			
COB *Site* Location			
Other *Recovery Site*			

COB/DR Site Functionality Matrix Form

Complete the following functionality matrix for each COB and/or DR site.

COB Site:

	Primary Recovery Site Location	Tertiary Recovery Site Location	Other Recovery Site Location
How many seats are needed? Business users/technicians			
Have emulator scripts been transferred?			
Have access control lists to remote hosts been revised to accommodate the new COB IP ranges?			

Have critical application and data been made available?			
Are production processes already running at this site?			
How long can this recovery site be functional?			
Is it a functional occupied site or functional dark space?			
Are there current agreements with necessary vendors and/or other company departments?			
Do existing SLAs of the IT DR plan support COB site users, equipment and business processes?			
What is the date of the last test at this recovery site?			

DR Site for Technologists:

	Primary Recovery Site Location	Tertiary Recovery Site Location	Other Recovery Site Location
How many workstations are needed?			
Are new passwords needed?			
Have emulator scripts been transferred?			
Have access control lists to remote hosts been revised to accommodate the new COB IP ranges?			
Have critical application and data been made available?			
How long can this recovery site be productive?			
Is it a functional occupied site or functional dark space?			
Are there current agreements with necessary vendors and/or other company departments?			
What is the date of the last test at this recovery site?			

Disaster Recovery Plan Type Checklist

- Is the plan focused on an alternate dark site?
- Is the plan set up for a parallel processing site?
- Is the plan a simple off-site data backup plan?
- Is the DR plan totally integrated with the COB plan?
- Is there a COB/DR training program?
- Have users and IT support personnel completed COB/DR training?
- Are the COB/DR plans accessible?

Comments: _____

DR/COB Awareness Training Checklist

- Is there a COB/DR awareness program?
- Are the plan principals aware of their assigned tasks in case of emergency?
- Are all employees aware of their role in the COB/DR plan?
- Have stakeholders rehearsed notification protocols?
- Have you set up a 24/7 toll-free number for rumor control and official information during an emergency?
- Have you created an e-mail (home e-mail addresses) distribution list?
- Do you have a current list of primary and alternate telephone numbers, pagers, etc.?
- Is the plan(s) stored in more than one place and off site?

Miscellaneous Considerations Checklist

- Is there additional information that should be brought to the attention of business management or COB/DR personnel?
- Add your own reminders.

Questionnaire Sign-off

Business Manager/Owner: _____ Date:_____

COB Manager: _____ Date:_____

DR Manager: _____ Date:_____

Risk Acceptance for Disaster Plan Deviations Form

Use this risk deviation form if you or one of your clients is unable to be compliant with DR/ COB standards. The organization (business) manager and the IT manager must sign off to accept the risk of noncompliance. *One department executive would likely not be able to accept the risk responsibility for another department or the entire organization without specific permission.*

I: General Information

      Date of Request: _____ Business Unit: _____

      Business Location: _____

      Requestor:

      Name: _____ Title: _____

      Telephone Number: _____ E-mail: _____

II: Request Type (Check One)

      Deviation ____ Additional requirement ____

III: What needs to be addressed?

      Section Rubric or Number: _____ Page #_____

      Section Requirements (be brief): _____

IV: Request Justification*

DEVIATION:

- Describe the deviation.
- What is the rationale for noncompliance (for example, technically unfeasible, cost impact, operational impact, time delay, etc.)?

ADDITIONAL REQUIREMENT:

- What is the description and rationale for the additional requirement?

INCLUDE:

- The risk (include all threats, exposures, and vulnerabilities) that will exist if this deviation is approved:
- All compensating controls currently implemented, including corrective actions planned to mitigate the risks identified in number III:
- Specify the expiration date for the request: _____

V: Organization Approvals

Name: _____   Title: _____

Organization: _____ Approval Date: _____

* *An approved Not Applicable/ Deviation /Additional Request Form is not valid after a determined period from the latest approval date noted in section V above. Resubmit the form after that time.*

DR/COB Test Planning Worksheet Form

Testing during the DR/COB site implementation and periodically after the build has been completed is essential. This template can be helpful to plan and execute a various testing methodologies.

Department and Process Name: _____

General Information:

- Indicate the type of test:

_ Phase ____ of _____ Plan.

- Alert pyramid tree prepared?
- Transfer production to: _____
- Test type:
  _ COB test   _ Technology DR test
- Conduct testing via a remote connection to the disaster site?
  _ Yes _ No
- Reason for the test:
  _ Periodic compliance: _ Retest of _____ (date)
  _ Recovery site change: _____ (date)
  _ Business operations change: _____ (date)
- Location of the test:

Address: _____ Floor/Suite: _____

City: _____State: _____ Zip Code: _____

- Location type:
  _ Primary _ Secondary _ Tertiary _ Remote: _____
- Anticipated test duration:
  _ Months: #____   _Weeks: #____ Days: #_____ Hours: #_____
- Testing schedule and participation:

Date of Test: _____   Time: _____

- Number of seats needed at COB site: _____
- Number of test participants scheduled: _____
- Number of dedicated support personnel _____
- Date of last similar test: _____
- Participating support teams:
  _ Audit _ Facilities _ Desktop/Network Support
  _ Other:
  I. _____

Testing Details:

What disaster situation does this test assume?

- The network with connectivity to the primary site
  _ is available _ not available
- List other assumptions.
  1. _____
  2. _____

Test Goals and Outcomes:

What are the goals and objectives of this test? What are the expected outcomes?

GOALS	OUTCOMES

Special Testing Situations:

- Noncritical business unit (if applicable)

Provide the following information if your business is considered noncritical and <u>will not partici-pate</u> in a COB test.

<u>Note:</u> *This option is not valid for all departments. Consult with your COB representative before selecting this option.*

What does your business unit or process do?
  1. _____

- Why is your function noncritical?
  1. _____
- Do other business units depend on your process?
  _ No _ Yes
- Transfer of function (if applicable):
- Has a successful "transfer of process" been completed in the past?
  _ No _Yes _____ (date)
- Indicate which facility and department will <u>receive</u> the transferred functions:

Department Name: _____

Department Location: _____

- List all processes to be transferred:
  1. _____

Attach additional pages if necessary

- Does a written service level agreement (SLA) exist?
- Has the document been approved by business and IT managers?
- Does it include the details of this transfer of function?
  _ Yes Date of the agreement: Date: _____
  _ No Why is an SLA not necessary? _____
- Does the receiving business unit have the appropriate number of staff to handle the anticipated volume of transferred functions?
- Need additional staff? _ Yes _ No
  How many? _____
  What type of personnel? _____

Business Test Coordinator_____
Technical Test Coordinator _____

Sign Off:
You should vet the information provided in this Test Planning Worksheet with a disaster recovery management team, including business and technology managers. In the event that any key aspect of this test should change (date, location, goals and accomplishments, etc.), notify all stakeholders.

Business Manager: _____
Technology Manager: _____

Date: _____

DR/COB Test Results Form

The importance of DR/COB testing and measurement of the results has been emphasized throughout the workbook. Use the following form as a testing metrics framework. Enhance the form to account for specific processes. Quantify as many activities as possible so you can calculate a complete metrics report.

Department Name: _____

General Information:

Indicate overall test results status:

Date of Test: _____ _ Successful _ Unsuccessful

Indicate the type of test performed:

_ Remote recovery site   _ Remote simulation

Indicate changes to test planning worksheet:

Has any testing information changed since you completed the last test planning worksheet (test location, scope of test, applications, etc.)?

_ No _ Yes (list below)

_____

Indicate test participation:

Test Date: _____ Start Time: _____ Finish Time: _____

Number of: Test participants: _____ Support participants: _____

Were other business units included in this test? _ No _ Yes (*list other units*)

_____

Were external service providers included in this test? _ No _ Yes
(*list providers*)

_____

Test Details:

In what type of environment was this test performed?

_ Simulated COB environment (usually done by remote access to COB site)

_ *Using production data*

_ Using dummy data

_ Start to end (*full cycle testing, start to finish*)

_ From _____ point to _____ point

- Only the following process: _____

_ Percentage of average daily volume tested. _____

_ Actual COB environment (users actually go to the COB site)

_ *Using production data (make sure to synchronize data sets)*
_ Using dummy data
_ End to end (full cycle testing, start to finish)
_ From _____ point to _____ point
_ Only the following process: _____
_ Percentage of average daily volume tested. _____

Were all tested processes successful?   _ Yes   _ No
Indicate all processes that tested <u>NOT SUCCESSFUL</u>:
Include the function name, risk exposure, and issue experienced:
1. _____ _ High _ Medium _ Low
Issue: _____
2. _____ _ High _ Medium _ Low
Issue:_____
   Add additional items or pages if necessary

Was a server restoration part of this test?   _ No   _ Yes
(*If yes*) Indicate server name and location: _____
What was restored on the server?
_ Operating system   _ Data _ Applications
Indicate the length of time needed for server restoration: _____
Is this restoration time = to, < or > than your COB pPlan estimate?
__ Equal to __ Less than __ Greater than
What was the time difference? _____
Were all applications recovered? _ Yes   _ No

Lessons Learned:

Indicate whether the following items were sufficient at the recovery site:

Seating Capacity	_ No	_ Yes
Parking	_ No	_ Yes
LAN Capacity	_ No	_ Yes
Environmental	_ No	_ Yes
Office Supplies	_ No	_ Yes
PCs, Printers	_ No	_ Yes
IT Services	_ No	_ Yes

List other unsatisfactory elements:

Special Testing Situations:

Remote Tests:

Indicate from where the remote test was conducted:

_ Home _ Primary Site _ Other _____

What did you not have that was necessary to test?

For transfer of process tests:

What processes were transferred? _____

Were all processes transferred successfully? _ Yes _ No

If no, indicate processes that were unsuccessful, and why:

Successful Test Results Sign-off:

General reminders:

- Update the test results section of your DR/COB plan with written results of this test. Refer to any supporting test documentation you have (screen prints, reports, etc.).
- Retain all supporting test documentation in accordance with the organization's record retention policy.

Unsuccessful Test Results Sign-off:

- Prepare a corrective action plan describing how the issue will be resolved, and forward a copy to the disaster management team soon after your test date.
- Complete a new test planning worksheet and forward a copy to disaster management.

Successful Test Sign-off Attestation:

This test provided an adequate representation of the critical processes of my business area. In the event that my business area was unable to perform processes as usual, I am confident that our continuity of business process will be sufficient to limit the losses of the organization, and to continue to provide products and/or services to internal and/or external customers with minimal interruption.

Business Manager: _____   Date: _____

Technology Manager: _____   Date: _____

Software and Application Information Collection Form

- Use this tool to collect information about applications the organization will need at the COB site.
- Be as granular as is necessary to insure that you represent all departments.
- Be aware that you may need to procure licenses for applications used at the DR/COB site.
- Applications generally need data to perform processes. Where will the data come from? Where will the data be hosted for COB?
- Have you thought about repatriating data sets from the COB site back to the primary site?

Department:
Submitted by:

Application Name	Software Type	OS Platform	Users Numbers	COB Migration Notes

Application Name	Data File Name	From Location	To Location

Replicate this template as needed.

User Data Information Collection Matrix Form

- Use this more detailed data set matrix to discover data content and directory structure that needs to be replicated at the COB site.
- Keep in mind that data points (directories) also need correct permissions granted to allow users access to their data.
- Do not forget that the COB environment data should be no less secure than your primary site data.
- Data owners are often departmental managers and may be different from data-users. You may need the data owner authorization to have a data-user access data.

Replicate this template as needed.

Application Name	Date Owner	Present Data Store Location	Data Store Location on COB Server	Data Migration Notes
Permission the following users to the COB data point listed above				

- Data owner authorization to permission user to data point:
- Never revise data permissions to users without explicit permission from the data owner.

Name: _____ Signature: _____ Date: _____

Multiple Projects Worksheet Sample

This form is useful if there are several departmental continuity of business projects at the same time

		Multiple Projects Status Tracking Report						
Status / Type I - 5	Rank I-100	Project Number	Project Name	Project Manager	Project Sponsor	Project Owner	Date Start	Date End
Active								
I	15	PR0001	A new project	Name	Name		03/27/xx	
4	34	PR1234	A new project	Name	Name			04/30/xx

Assigned But Not Started								
5	4	PR2345	A new project	Name				06/01/xx
4	I	PR9876	A new project	Name				11/01/xx
I	13	PR7767	A new project	Name				
Unassigned								
3	11	PR7865	A new project	Name			03/31/xx	
4	76	PR2394	A new project	Name				
3	32	PR5673	A new project	Name				

Type Legend

1. Operations
2. COB/DR
3. Audit
4. Mandatory
5. Optional

Project Planning Template—Sample #1

There are many ways to organize a project-planning document. This particular template is a simple, modular form that may be useful to construct a detailed plan template.

Stakeholders and Team Members

Stakeholders	Telephone	Cell Phone	E-mail Address	Location
Project Sponsor				
Project Lead				
Project Advisor				
Team Member				
Team Member				
Team Member				
Stakeholder				
Stakeholder				

Document History

Version	Date	Comment/Changes from Prior Version

Project Goals

Goal Name	#	Goal Purpose

Goal—Tasks—Attributions—Time Lines—Solutions

Goal Name					
Business Requirement					
Task Name	Task Description	Assigned to	Date Due	Comments/Status	

Documented Resources

Designation	Documentation Location

Testing

No.	Test Conditions	Expected Results	Actual Results	Reference

Note: Cut and paste sections of this template as many times as necessary to create your template.

Project Planning Simplest Template—Sample #2

An abbreviated form with only four items such as indicated below is useful for tracking and publishing project progress for meetings. If the form is a Microsoft Word document, most stakeholders will be able to view it. Regardless of the format of project tracking forms, the elements of every tracking form list should include at a bare minimum:

- Item or task
- Attribution—who is responsible for the task
- Dates—start date and expected end date
- Notes

You can keep a more detailed and visually pleasing report with the inclusion of dependencies and costs in a commercial project-management software package such as Microsoft Project.

It is sometimes useful to commence a project plan with simple high-level tasks on a time line tracking form, and then, as more details are discovered, segue into a more detailed report like the **Detailed Project Plan Template Sample #3** shown below.

Detailed Project Plan Template—Sample #3

Although this plan is quite detailed, it is not complete. However, it does show many of the considerations that make up the build of a DR/COB site or, for that matter, the build of a primary production site.

Some of the items in this template may not be necessary for a small organization.

Project Name:	Business & Department DR/COB PROJECT #3333 *PROJECT REQUEST #: 999999* Cost Codes: xxxxxx. *LAN INFRASTRUCTURE EQUIPMENT Purchase Order #: 11111* *WAN INFRASTRUCTURE EQUIPMENT PO#: 22222* PC/SERVER EQUIPMENT PO#: 33333 ADDITIONAL PERSONNEL PO#: 44444
Remote COB Site Info:	*Business Remote Site Contact: Jimmy James, Site Manager, 123 Remote Road, Away Place, MT, xxxxx-xxxx, Tele: xxx-xxx-xxxx, Location Code: COB2345*
Objective: To bring business remote DR/COB site into compliance with best practice.	General Goals and Milestones: 1) Project initiating functions concluded (Pre-engagement, Engagement) 2) Project planning processes concluded (Discovery, Design) 3) Project executing activities concluded (Implementation) 4) Project controlling functions concluded (Metrics, Monitoring, Testing, and Reporting) 5) Project Closing Functions Concluded (Close)
Lead Project Manager:	Tele: As of: 07/29/xx
Target Completion Date:	Original: 07/30/xx Revised: 07/28/xx

DONE	Task #	Task Description	Who Do	Done Date	Status Notes
X	I	COMPLETE ENGAGEMENT ACTIVITIES		06/15/xx	Complete
X	I.I	Accept initial business requirement document		05/15/xx	Complete
X	I.2	Suggest metrics elements		05/30/xx	Pending
X	I.3	Confirm sponsor in writing		05/01/xx	Complete
X	I.4	Authority gateways		06/15/xx	Complete
X	I.4.I	Procure sponsor sign-off to proceed with project		06/01/xx	Complete
X	I.4.2	Procure high-level cost code to allow budget tracking		06/17/xx	Complete

X	1.5	Open a big business service request for personnel expense attribution		05/06/xx	Complete
X	1.6	Compile a stakeholders list and solicit participation (names and roles)			Complete—Distributed
X	1.7	Finalize core operations/engineering team		05/07/xx	Complete
X	1.8	Complete and distribute a communications matrix (names and contact information)		05/08/xx	Complete—Distributed
X	1.9	Establish reoccurring conference time and place, including dial-in #		05/20/xx	Complete—Distributed
	2	**COMPLETE DISCOVERY ACTIVITIES**		06/30/xx	IN PROCESS
	2.0.0	**Server Discovery**			
	2.0.1	Data file servers			
	2.0.2	Fax servers			
	2.0.3	FTP servers			
	2.0.4	Print servers			
	2.0.5	Software application servers (backend client server, etc.)			
	2.0.6	Application distribution servers			
	2.0.7	**Application Discovery**			
	2.0.8	Identify applications			
	2.0.9	Identify needed Web sites			
	2.0.10	Substitute applications			
	2.0.11	*Identify host applications*			
	2.0.12	Identify clientside applications connecting to host			
	2.0.13	Evaluate application update opportunity			
	2.0.14	Test evaluation applications			
	2.0.15	Promote evaluation applications to production			
	2.0.16	*Discovery is necessary to permission users to new production applications*			
	2.0.20	**Other Discovery**			
	2.0.21	E-mail discovery—COB users to mail server			
	2.0.21.1	Public folders—shared data locations			
	2.0.22	LAN printers (location of print server)			
	2.0.22.1	Local print queues			
	2.0.22.2	Remote source IP printers (e.g., headquarters printouts)			
	2.0.22.3	Personal printers (are they needed?)			
	2.0.23	Network discovery (circuits, routers, etc.)			

	2.0.24	Emulator scripts (3279 emulators, etc.)			
	2.0.25	Terminal server sessions (firewall changes)			
	2.0.26	Passwords			
	2.0.27	Firewall issues (ACLs)			
X	2.1	Photograph remote COB space for design team		06/19/xx	Use digital camera
X	2.2	Define existing LAN/WAN/desktop DR site equipment		05/30/xx	
X	2.2.1	What existing equipment stays?		05/30/xx	
X	2.2.2	What existing applications stay? Additional applications?		05/30/xx	Submit "Applications by Department" matrix
X	2.2.3	Tech plate and PDS solution		06/12/xx	
X	2.3	Design WAN circuit and router requirements		06/19/xx	
X	2.3.1	WAN circuits order		05/20/xx	Complete
	2.3.3	Scope data size and transfer time for critical file transfer from primary server to COB servers. Take only what is needed.		06/19/xx	Send an e-mail to managers inquiring about critical files. Collect and collate the files.
	2.3.4	Order circuits from the primary site to the COB site and from the COB site to WAN targets.		06/19/xx	
	2.4	Review LAN/WAN equipment requirements for new network.		06/19/xx	Include DSU/CSU, router/probes, encryptors, patch panels, racks, cabinet, cables, and patch cords.
	2.4.1	Create BOM		06/19/xx	
	2.4.2	Access memory requirements for existing PC at COB site		06/19/xx	Most of the PCs need memory upgrades.

X	2.5	Assess DR software requirements		06/19/xx	Productivity suite as well as the inclusion of any software necessary for special processes.
	2.6	**PROFILE MEETINGS WITH BUSINESS HEADS**			
X	2.6.1	Collect user profile information			
X	2.6.2	Existing apps placed on profile			
X	2.7	Analyze user profile information			
X	2.7.1	Application substitution and deletion process			
	2.8	Review user profiles with business managers and individual users		07/15/xx	
	2.9	User profile sign-off by business heads		07/15/xx	
	2.10	Create project implementation schedule		06/30/xx	
	2.11	Create and submit site budget		06/30/xx	Pending determination of project scope. BRD
	3	**COMPLETE DESIGN ACTIVITIES**		**06/30/05**	**PENDING**
	3.1	Design LAN/WAN solution		06/30/xx	Completed the COB site design for two departments. Investigating expansion.
	3.1.1	Site survey—sufficient space?		06/19/xx	Install two additional cabinets for all required LAN/WAN equipment. Decision to build out infrastructure to accommodate all departments is pending.

	3.1.2	Photograph the site		06/19/xx	Photographed the site on 07/13/xx. Label and copy the jpeg files to post them.
	3.1.2	Finalize hardware requirements for LAN/WAN/desktop		06/19/xx	Completed—list posted. Investigating expansion.
	3.1.3	Order memory upgrades for existing COB site PCs		06/19/xx	Most of the PCs are business standard and will need memory upgrades.
	3.1.4	Order encryptors for the COB circuits		06/19/xx	Need six line encryptors point to point from DR site to NYC.
	3.1.5	Order WAN circuits		0619/xx	Sent an e-mail to WAN vendors to get circuits set up.
X	3.1.6	Determine if probes are necessary		06/12/xx	Are monitoring probes necessary to monitor the equipment after installation?
	3.1.7	Order WAN equipment (DSUs, encryptors, etc.)		06/19/xx	Assist from the telephone company?
	3.2	Design cabling solution [PDS]		06/19/xx	Cable bundles will need to be installed between switch and tech room patch panes.
	3.2.1	Order #100—100' Cat5 patch cables		06/19/xx	Order cords.

	3.3	Design software solution		06/18/xx	Stipulate what software will be added to existing user profiles.
	3.3.1	Upgrade OS		05/31/xx	If necessary
	3.3.2	Test software solution.		06/30/xx	
	3.4	Finalize implementation plan		06/19/xx	Waiting for decision on project scope revision.
	3.5	Finalize all design drawings		06/19/xx	Engineering will do the elevations.
	3.6	Order technical temp for COB conversion.		06/19/xx	Request a technical temp to help with the implementation work at COB site.
	3.6.1	Finalize equipment needs		06/19/xx	Track the equipment order.
	3.7	**Hardware Order Process**			
	3.7.1	Create server order			
	3.7.2	Get management sign-off			
	3.7.3	Get tech finance sign-off			
	3.7.7	Create desktop order			
	3.7.8	Get management sign-off			
	3.7.9	Get tech finance sign-off			
	3.7.12	Create printer order			
	3.7.13	Get management sign-off			
	3.7.14	Get tech finance sign-off			
	3.7.16	PO cut			
	3.7.18	Analyze existing laptops			
	3.7.19	Determine laptop needs			
	3.7.20	Create laptop order			
	3.7.21	Get management sign-off			
	3.7.22	Get tech finance sign-off			
	3.7.25	Move three cabinets from primary site to COB site to hold new equipment			Primary site warehouse truck will deliver them to COB site.
	3.7.26	Order power hookups for the new equipment			Provide power requirements to utility.

X	3.7.3	Finalize gap (risk) analysis primary site to COB site			The implementation will occur in batch cut-overs while the existing site remains in production.
	3.8	Submit gap analysis, final design and final budget to sponsor			
	3.9	Procure sponsor sign-off to proceed with implementation			
X	3.10	Design control metrics matrix			
X	3.10.1	Finalize measure of performance elements (MOP)			
	3.11	Design additional report matrix (templates)			
	4	**COMPLETE IMPLEMENTA-TION ACTIVITIES**			PENDING
	4.1	Demarc—WAN T1 circuits all elements			
	4.2	Install LAN/WAN equipment			
	4.2.1	Install cabinets for equipment	06/30/xx		
	4.2.2	Install power for cabinets	06/30/xx		
	4.2.3	Install equipment in cabinets	06/30/xx		
	4.2.4	Configure DSU/CSU and encryptors	07/15/xx		
	4.2.5	Configure routers	07/15/xx		
	4.2.6	Configure distribution switches	07/15/xx		
	4.2.7	Extend Demarced circuits to DSUs	07/15/xx		
	4.2.8	Patching activities T1 to CSU/DSU Switches to encryptors and routers Patch panels to switches Desktops to tech-plates	07/15/xx		
	4.2.9	Build servers	07/15/xx		
	4.2.10	Patch servers to routers	07/15/xx		
	4.2.11	Build desktops	07/30/xx		
	4.2.12	Patch desktops from patch panels to distribution switches (tech plates already exist)	07/15/xx		
	4.3	Procure temporary tech person for implementation help.			Get approval
	4.4.0	*Server Build Process (PDC, BDC, Print, Data)*			
	4.4.1	Network ready (manually enter date)			
	4.4.2	Servers Received			
	4.4.3	Build servers			

	4.4.4	Obtain MTR rack space			
	4.4.5	Submit patching request			
	4.4.6	Publish IPs			
	4.4.7	Server installed in MTR			
	4.4.8	Server patching complete			
	4.4.9	Server brought online			
	4.4.10	Work with backup group on data retention for all servers			
	4.4.11	Publish all servers			
	4.4.12	Install monitoring			
	4.4.14	Complete user profiles			
	4.4.15	Server Q&A complete			
	4.4.16	Server turned over to production			
	4.4.17	Documentation completed			
	4.4.19	Patching and workstation layout			
	4.4.20	Workstations received			
	4.4.21	Workstations built			
	4.4.23	DHCP configured and tested			
	4.4.24	Workstations deployed and patched			
	4.4.26	Workstations deployment completed and tested on the LAN and WAN			
	4.4.27	Workstation final walk through			
	4.4.28	*Workstation Recovery/Rebuild*			
	4.4.29	Recover old workstations			
	4.4.30	*Rebuild recovered workstations for redeployment*			
	4.4.32	*Laptop Build*			
	4.4.33	Identify critical laptop users			
	4.4.34	Build first 10 laptops			
	4.4.35	Build additional laptops			
	4.4.36	*Create Printing Environment*			
	4.4.37	Receive printers			
	4.4.38	Printers put into locations			
	4.4.39	IP address entered into white pages			
	4.4.40	Printers completed and on the network			
	4.4.41	Print queues created and tested			
	4.4.42	*Complete User Environment*			
	4.4.43	Review of user IDs are complete			
	4.4.45	Create necessary new IDs			
	4.4.46	Create home directories on COB servers			
	4.4.47	Create home directories shares on COB servers			
	4.4.48	Create home directories permissions on COB servers			

	4.4.49	Create group directories on COB servers			
	4.4.50	Create group shares on COB servers			
	4.4.51	Create group permissions on COB servers			
	4.4.52	Give user access to core productivity applications			
	4.4.53	Permission users to use printing environment			
	4.4.55	*Data Migration*			
	4.4.56	Analyze data migration from existing servers			
	4.4.57	Create from-to data documents			
	4.4.58	Create data migration scripts			
	4.4.59	Build data migration server			
	4.4.60	Copy user home directories from primary to COB location servers and sync data periodically			
	4.4.61	Copy group share directories to COB location servers and sync data periodically			
	4.4.62	Final migration to COB servers by tape or copying data over the wire			
	4.4.64	*User Acceptance Testing*			
	4.4.65	Create testing lab ("test bed")			
	4.4.66	Set up workstations for testing			
	4.4.67	Create user checkout worksheets			
	4.4.68	Schedule user testing with business			
	4.4.69	Conduct testing			
	4.4.70	Retest as necessary			
	4.4.71	*Access (or other end-user) Databases*			Note: Update specific data stores from only ONE place at a time.
	4.4.72	Data store identification from users			
	4.4.73	Copy data to swing server			
	4.4.74	Test relink of databases			
	4.4.75	Final relink test of databases			
	4.4.76	*User Mail Migration*			
	4.4.77	Identify BlackBerry and other mail device users			
	4.4.78	Creation of MS Outlook PST files			
	4.4.79	Work with MS exchange management group on conversions			
	4.4.80	Get user IDs list to the exchange administrator			

	4.4.81	Create PST file migration script			
	4.4.82	Copy PST files to home directories			
	4.4.83	Verify link to PST file in MS Outlook			
	4.4.84	*Lotus Notes*			
	4.4.85	Identify servers			
	4.4.86	Identify remote users			
	4.4.87	Create international IDs if necessary			
	4.4.88	Notify all remote users of DNS and IP changes			
	4.4.89	Install/configure notes for users			
	4.4.90	Test functionality of notes with users			
	4.4.92	**Implementation Day**			
	4.4.93	Sunday test before "Day One"			
	4.4.94	Document and label "hot cut" equipment			
	4.4.95	Create final user checkout worksheets			
	4.4.96	Coordinate user checkout (S)			
	4.4.97	Prepare weekend coverage list/weekend responsibilities document			
	4.4.98	Post all documentation on Web site			
	5	**COMPLETE CONTROL FUNCTIONS**		09/25/xx	PENDING
	5.1	LAN connectivity testing		07/30/xx	
	5.2	Wan connectivity testing		07/30/xx	
	5.3	UAT (user acceptance testing) end to End		07/30/xx	
	5.4	Complete and submit interim project metrics		07/30/xx	
	5.5	Complete stipulated interim reports		07/30/xx	
	5.6	Finalize process control manual		07/30/xx	
	6	**COMPLETE PROJECT CLOSE ACTIVITIES**		09/30/xx	
	6.1	Dispose of legacy equipment		09/30/xx	
	6.2	Finalize reoccurring DR test dates		09/30/xx	
	6.3	Submit final metrics and reports)		09/30/xx	
	6.31	Lessons learned		09/30/xx	
	6.32	Quantify end state data from gap analysis		09/30/xx	
	6.4	Submit actual budget		09/30/xx	
	6.5	Notify all stakeholders and users of project close		09/30/xx	

Project Planning Document—Sample #4

Here is still another style of project planning template. It includes a sample **bill of materials** [BOM] listing necessary purchases. Add, subtract, or revise document modules as desired to fit your situation.

Project Name:	
Team Lead:	
Project Code:	
Expense Code:	
Project Priority:	
Level 3 Capital Expense:	
Level 3 Maintenance Cost:	
Sponsoring Business:	
Management Sponsor:	
Department Sponsor:	
Document Name:	
Author:	
Contributors:	
Revision Date:	

General Contact Information

Function	Name	Phone
Team Lead		
Sponsor		
Engineer		
Etc.		

Project Scope

- Write a complete list of all included deliverables—tasks and goals.
- As much as possible, also write those things that will not be completed by this project.

Justification of the Project

Why is the project necessary? (Embed documented evidence here.) If this project does not happen on a timely basis, what is the risk to the organization?

1.
2.

Project Prioritization

☐   BUSINESS AS USUAL   ☐ IMPORTANT   ☐ CRITICAL

Explain:

Time Lines

Milestone	Scheduled
Engage Project Start	
Engage Project Complete	
Define (Discover) Start	
Define Project Complete	
Design Start	
Design Complete	
Implementation Start	
Build Complete	
Close Project Complete	

Technical Design:

Embed the technical design document here.

Special Considerations:

Attach unusual or especially challenging situations.

BOM (Bill of Materials Form)

The BOM is a planning document that lists project purchases such as equipment, software, personnel, or any other items that need to in the budgeted. **Keep in mind that any software used in the DR/COB site must be licensed.**

Part Number	Description	Price US$	Quantity	Total Price
Part Name:				
Part Name:				
Part Name:				
Part Name:				
Part Name:				

Are Wan Circuits Required?

☐ YES.   Are the requirements and procurement contained in the plan?

☐ NO.   WAN circuits are not required.

Implementation Plans:

Embed granular (detailed) implementation plan here. **Include back-out steps in case of plan failure.**

Project Planning Milestone Document—SAMPLE #5

This milestone document is the fifth in the series of project planning templates. Because it is condensed and allows the project manager and the stakeholders to see a high-level progress overview of the project, it is a very useful document. It also shows how the project flows against a time line. Once these milestones and dates are agreed on, the creation of a more granular plan is possible.

HIGH-LEVEL MILESTONES AGAINST AN APPROXIMATE TIME LINE PLAN REVISION DATE 08/11/xx
DRAFT VERSION: # TECHNICAL CONTACT:
ORIGANAL ESTIMATED COMPLETION DATE: 05/30/xx REVISED ESTIMATED PROJECT COMPLETION DATE: 12/31/xx

#	MILESTONE Tasks	Who Do	Done By Date	Notes
1	EQUIPMENT STAGING SPACE PREPARED		06/01/xx	
2	PROJECT PERSONNEL HIRED AND TRAINED		08/01/xx	
3	PCs / PRINTERS ORDERED, DELIVERED, UNBOXED AND BUILT		09/30/xx	
3.1	Ordered		05/01/xx	Delivery 08/15/xx
3.2	Unboxed		08/15/xx	Need 4 temp help
3.3	Built		09/30/xx	Six week PC build
4	SERVERS ORDERED DELIVERED, UNBOXED AND BUILT		10/15/xx	
4.1	Ordered		04/01/xx	Delivery 07/10/xx
4.2	Unboxed		07/10/xx	Temp help
4.3	Built		10/15/xx	
5	ROUTERS ORDERED, DELIVERED, UNBOXED AND BUILT		08/01/xx	
5.1	Ordered		04/01/xx	Delivery 07/10/xx
5.2	Unboxed		07/10/xx	Temp help
5.3	Built		08/01/xx	Ready to connect when WAN circuits complete
#	MILESTONE Tasks	Who Do	Done By Date	Notes
6	SWITCHES ORDERED, DELIVERED, UNBOXED AND BUILT		08/01/0xx	

#	Tasks	Who Do	Done By Date	Notes
6.1	Ordered		04/01/xx	Delivery 7/10/xx
6.2	Unboxed		07/10/xx	Temp Help
6.3	Built		08/01/xx	Ready to connect when WAN circuits are done.
7	**TECHNICAL SPACES COMPLETED [CER, TECH, PBX, DEMARC]**		**06/15/xx**	**CRITICAL PATH ITEM**
7.1	Construction checklist for technical equipment areas		06/15/xx	*See Construction Checklist for Technical Equipment Areas*
8	**WAN CIRCUITS CONNECTIVITY COMPLETED**		**08/01/xx**	**CRITICAL PATH ITEM**
8.1	Router to router connectivity		08/01/xx	
9	**ROUTERS, SWITCHES, SERVERS RACKED AND CONNECTED**		09/25/xx	
9.1	Racked		06/05/xx	
9.2	Built/Connected		09/25/xx	
#	**MILESTONE** **Tasks**	**Who Do**	**Done By Date**	**Notes**
10	**USER CUBES AND OFFICES COMPLETED**		**10/15/xx**	**CRITICAL PATH ITEM**
10.1	200		08/28/xx	Dependent on facility preparation
10.2	200		09/11/xx	This schedule can also follow the UAT schedule
10.3	200		09/25/xx	
11	**PCs DISTRIBUTED TO DESKTOPS**		09/25/xx	
11.1	200		08/28/xx	Dependent on facility preparation
11.2	200		09/11/xx	This schedule can also follow the UAT schedule
11.3	200		09/25/xx	
12	**MIGRATION OF DATA AND APPS TO NEW SERVERS COMPLETE**		09/25/xx	
13	**UAT COMPLETED**		10/15/xx	
14	**TAPE BACKUP SOLUTION INSTALLED**		10/15/xx	
15	**USER MIGRATION UAT COMPLETED**		11/30/xx	
15.1	Phase one		09/11/xx	Nine weeks
15.2	Phase two		09/18/xx	
15.3	Phase three		09/25/xx	
15.4	Phase four		10/02/xx	
15.5	Phase five		10/09/xx	
15.6	Phase six		10/16/xx	
15.7	Phase seven		10/23/xx	
15.8	Phase eight		11/13/xx	
16	**PROJECT CLOSE CLEAN UP**		12/31/xx	

Partial Construction Checklist for Technical Equipment Areas

This partial construction checklist reflects some of the tasks needed to prepare a DR/COB site or indeed any new technical area. It is not without omissions. Moreover, in view of different levels of business criticality and resources, some of the items may not prove to be necessary or cost effective. See the items as potential concerns.

- Concrete flooring sealed
- Fire retardant coating has been applied on beams and ceiling above all technical areas
- Fire-rated hard walls around the perimeter of technical areas finished
- Installation of interior security fencing to partition and compartmentalize various functional domains, such as the computer equipment, demarc, PBX, and tech room (wiring closet)
- Exterior wall steel doors at entrances to all discrete technical areas with approved access security systems installed
- Card key or other cipher technology locks with central monitoring system installed on all limited-access area doors
- All racks and cabinets for technical equipment bolted to raised floor and/or concrete subfloor
- Plywood installed on technical area walls as wall-field for cable plant installation
- Electric distribution panels installed from two separate electrical sources
- Electrical conduit installed in the ceiling or under floors
- PDUs (power distribution units) racked and all conduit and wiring to support installation of PDU units installed
- A system for notifying the technology teams implemented in advance for any scheduled interruption of power to the tech rooms
- Portals for cables cut through concrete floors
- Duplicated and physically separated ingress access points for copper and fiber optic communications lines
- Conduits (interbuilding and intrabuilding) for copper and fiber optic communications lines are installed
- Twelve-inch raised floors installed
- Conduits or trays for copper and fiber PDS below raised floors installed in the equipment room and user areas
- Conduits, ladders or trays for copper and fiber PDS installed above equipment in equipment room and user areas
- Premises distribution system [PDS] media pulled and tested from tech room to workstations
- Fire and/or smoke detection both above ceiling and below raised floors installed

- Fire alarms and fire command stations installed
- Fire suppression equipment installed in ceiling or under floor plenum (nonplenum spaces may not need fire suppression)
- Water detection equipment installed below raised floors
- A cooling plant installed that is adequate to support cooling needs for equipment in the computer equipment, demarc, PBX, and tech (wiring closet) areas
- All ceiling ductwork completed
- Drip pans placed under HVAC [heating and air conditioning] units
- Room lighting, including emergency lighting, installed and tested
- All ceiling water lines routed away from technical areas equipment (exception may be where fire code requires water sprinklers for fire suppression)
- Drop ceiling installed
- All technical areas cleaned to a high degree (dust free)

Signing this section authorizes the project manager to commence the build phase, including submission of required purchase requests for the materials listed under the Level 3 budget section and charge the expense codes as allocated.

Business Approval

Name	Date Approved	Comments
Customer (High Level)		
Customer (Mid-manager)		
Customer (Supervisor)		

Technology Approval

Name	Date Approved	Approval Number
Technology (Regional Manager)		
Technology (Site Manager)		

Network Diagrams Section

Embed revised network diagrams here.

Identify and list all change records that were the result of this project.

Change	Status (Successful, Closed with Issues, etc.)	Notes (If issues, identify how the issue was resolved.)

Project Build (As-built) Section

An "as-built document" is a final rendering of exactly what was implemented as differentiated from what was planned to be implemented.

Embed as-built documents here.

Remote DR/COB Site Handover Approval

Name	Date Approved	Comments
Technical Operations Manager		
Business Management		

Project Completion and Feedback—Sample Form

Project Time Lines

Milestone	Actual Date
Build Start	
Build Complete	
Closure Complete	
Etc. (Add as many as appropriate)	

Cost Assessment Spreadsheet

A cost assessment spreadsheet records the final project costs, identifies the deviation from the original costs estimated, and, if applicable, provides an explanation of why the costs deviated.

One Time/Capital	Final Estimate	Project Actual	Deviation (Esti-mate—Ac-tual)	Comments
TOTAL				
Ongoing Expenses (Maintenance/Circuits/etc.)	Final Estimate	Project Actual	Deviation (Esti-mate—Ac-tual)	Comments
TOTAL				

Were deliverables fulfilled? (If No, provide an explanation):

YES NO

☐ ☐   Was the project well defined?

☐ ☐   Was the project well designed?

☐ ☐   Did the implementation of the project meet design expectations?

☐ ☐   Did the project time line and cost constraints meet design expectations?

☐ ☐   Were project-closing documents (as built, final budget, etc.) completed and submitted on time?

Project Completion Sign-off

It is required that appropriate customer management and the technology team sign off on project completion.

Business Sign-off

Name	Date Approved	Signature
Customer		
Business Security/COB Officer		

Technology Team Approval

Name	Date Approved	Signature

Customer Satisfaction Form for the IT Team

Distribute to client organization users. Average scores to get a team satisfaction metric.

Sponsoring Business:
Business Area: **Business Contact:**
Project Name: **Project Code:**

PLEASE RATE THE INFORMATION TECHNOLOGY STAFF:

1 = POOR   5 = EXCELLENT

Overall experience working with the information technology staff during this project	☐ I ☐ 2 ☐ 3 ☐ 4 ☐ 5
Ability to fulfill the **requirements of the project**	☐ I ☐ 2 ☐ 3 ☐ 4 ☐ 5
Response time to address migration issues	☐ I ☐ 2 ☐ 3 ☐ 4 ☐ 5
Response time to **solve migration issues**	☐ I ☐ 2 ☐ 3 ☐ 4 ☐ 5
Ability to **fulfill budget requirements** (if relevant)	☐ I ☐ 2 ☐ 3 ☐ 4 ☐ 5
Ability to **fulfill time line requirements**	☐ I ☐ 2 ☐ 3 ☐ 4 ☐ 5

Additional comments:

Summary of Chapter 5

- Forms should serve useful purposes.
  - One form does not fit all situations.
  - Tailor the forms in this workbook to the needs of a particular situation.
- Some of the forms in this workbook are amenable to a large facility. However, the information collated via these forms is applicable in some part to most DR/COB situations large or small.

Definition of Terms

Information technology is fraught with a stupefying number of esoteric terms and acronyms that can make it very difficult for a nontechnical person to understand a conversation with a technologist. Below are a few of the many concepts and terms used in DR/COB projects and this workbook.

ACL = Access Control List

Access control lists are an integral part of certain operating and file systems. For example, the list might contain a list of IPs, user names or other designators that can access whatever is that the ACL is protecting. Think of an ACL as a filter giving permission to only an appropriate, pre-determined user or device. DR/COB plans must insure that work done at a new location is reflected in the ACL of mainframe hosts.

Adds, Moves, and Changes

"Adds, moves and changes" refers to the activities surrounding the "restacking" or moving of individual users or departments from here to there.

Alert Pyramid

An alert pyramid is a collection of DR/COB plan participants organized in a hierarchical fashion by department and/or function. The person at the top of a section contacts the individuals below them on the list using one of several possible communications modalities. When the contact list is completed, the top person reports contact success or failure to the person above in the organizational tree. Test metrics are collected and reviewed to assess plan functionality and to insure that contact information is current.

Alternate COB Site

An alternate COB site is a place that is already being used but, in case of an emergency at the primary site, employees already in place or users from the primary site will carry on critical production. Sometimes the alternate COB site is also used as a "parallel production site" or "split production site" where critical processes are done in "real time" all the time in anticipation of potential disaster.

Application Build

Like a technical site build, an application build describes the completion and details of a software application.

As Built Documents

"As built" documents are those design schematics that are drawn up after the project has been implemented. Changes to the original design documents to accommodate unexpected situations encountered during the implementation phase are common. The reason for "as built" documentation is to reflect exactly how the project was finally constructed. These documents are invaluable for the maintenance team.

Attribution

In the context of project management, the word "attribution" is sometime used as a substitute for the word "assignment." The meaning of both words indicates that someone has been made responsible for a particular task.

Backup Tapes

Backup tape systems allow selective data sets to be recorded and tracked in a specialized hard-drive based database directory. The physical tapes are then cycled off site and saved in a safe place for later retrieval.

Data backups are sometimes recorded incrementally each day for six days of the week. Incremental data backups record only new or changed files. A full data backup is accomplished on the seventh day.

Periodically (each day is advisable), the tapes should be removed from the recorder and taken off site. Store them in a secure climate controlled space. The physical tapes should be labeled and logged. The log record should contain information about data contents and backup times.

Follow the manufacturer's instructions regarding the tapes' shelf life and the number of times they can be reused. Backup tapes are usually machine- and backup-software specific, so insure that you have an alternate tape machine and data recovery servers in case your primary tape machine and data servers might be destroyed in a disaster.

BAU = Business as Usual

BAU represent those usual day-to-day production processes that are not extraordinary.

Bit Level Data Replication

While some replication software will back up data words, files or even larger data pieces, copying every bit in real time to another destination insures an absolutely up-to-date backup data set should the primary data set be destroyed.

BOM = Bill of Materials

A bill of materials is a document that lists and defines equipment and services with their cost.

Best Practice

Best practice is an agreement among professionals within a field of discipline concerning the most advantageous way to handle processes or situations.

Break and Fix Services

During the maintenance phase of a completed DR/COB project, the IT service team must offer the users "break and fix service." If a process or computer is not working, the technical staff must remedy the situation. Break and fix services network software exists that allows a user to log a repair or service ticket and track its completion.

BRD = Business Requirements Document

The BRD defines project goals, scope, methods, time line, and costs. It either is or serves as a basis for a contract between a sponsoring organization and the project manager or vendor organization.

Build

A build is a completed technical site attendant with the details of the job; e.g., "Is the site build complete?"

Burnout

Workers experience "burnout" when they are overworked over a long period of time. The psychological condition is akin to depression and can adversely affect productivity. Burnout can be exacerbated by assigning a worker responsibility without the authority or resources to accomplish the tasks.

CAP = Corrective Action Plan

A corrective action plan is that plan that addresses discovered deficits in a business process. The plan stipulates the issue and sets forth actions against a time line and personnel to accomplish remediation. A CAP is often the result of a gap analysis.

COB = Continuity of Business

A continuity of business plan by an organization elucidates answers to questions concerning how the organization will maintain productivity in the face of a disaster.

Compensating Control

A compensating control is a temporary process implemented to mediate the risk of an identified threat to the computing environment. A compensating control is usually followed by a corrective action plan to permanently fix the issue.

Confidential Nondisclosure Agreement

Confidentiality agreements are called several different things, including proprietary information contracts, nondisclosure agreements or trade secret agreements. The idea is that an outsider signing this kind of contract promises not to divulge information that is owned by the contracting company.

CPI = Critical Path Item

A CPI is a task within the project plan that, if not completed on a timely basis, will hold up the project. A CPI task undone is a "show stopper."

Dark Site

A dark site is a DR/COB site where a complete working computing infrastructure has been set up and made ready to use in case of a disaster. Except for testing, there are no users at this site unless a disaster is declared or during a COB test. See "Alternate COB Site."

Data Directory

A data directory is created on an internal backup machine hard drive. The directory holds information about file names and times recorded. The database makes it easy to retrieve or recover a particular file for a user.

Data Mirroring

A data mirror is an exact copy of a data set.

Deliverables

This term is used in project management. It simply refers to the tasks that need to be done by someone. Usually a time frame or due date is attached to a deliverable.

Demarc = Demarcation Point

The demarc is the place within a site where the telephone or cable company terminates its service line(s). The communication equipment within the site is connected to the outside world at the demarc location.

Dependencies

Dependencies are those tasks in a plan that are subordinate to and dependent on a prior task. Without the completion of the dependent task, the primary task cannot be completed.

DR = Disaster Recovery

Disaster recovery is the phrase most commonly used by IT organizations that sets forth their technical plan to provide support for a COB plan. The term "disaster recovery" is also often used interchangeably with "continuity of business."

Down Time

The phrase "down time" refers to the period of time that production is halted.

Drive Mappings

A drive mapping is expressed by assigning a letter (A-Z) to represent the virtual or logical location of a storage location or data set. The drive mapping points to a physical location on some kind of media within the computer or network.

Elevations

When used in the context of a server or communications room build, elevations are the drawings that show the front dimensions of the racks and cabinets in a "technical room" with the devices installed.

Emulator Session Files

It is common in large organizations that local PCs are used to access (create a session with) a remote mainframe host computer. Mainframes that require "client-host" devices like dumb terminals that are no longer in service can be accessed by PCs running emulation software that allows the mainframe to recognize the session. Emulator software generally needs a small data file to help identify the user and to point the device to the correct IP address. These "session files" must be replicated on DR/COB PCs.

Enterprise Computing

Enterprise computing refers to the equipment and processes required for wide area network system computing. Large corporations that have global facilities require enterprise computing resources. Enterprise Computing is differentiated from local—usually one-site—computing systems.

Firewall

In the computing world, a "firewall" is a software barrier that prevents uninvited packets of information from passing into the network or the computer.

FTE = Full Time Equivalent

An FTE is a worker that works a full workweek—usually calculated at forty hours per week. When calculating the cost of an FTE, make sure to include all employee or contractor expenses. Employees usually receive benefits that in many companies can add 30 percent to the base wage. Consultants or temporary workers usually work for independent contractors who mark up wages to cover worker benefits, administration, and their profit.

Hot Button

The phrase "hot button" is used to represent particular issues that management considers to be critical. The discovery and attention to hot button issues is important to garner the interest and support of management.

IS = Information Systems

"IS" is often used interchangeably with "IT."

IT = Information Technology

Information technology refers to an industry that concerns itself with computing and communications technologies.

LAN = Local Area Network

A local area network provides file and print services, usually from the demarc inward. It includes workstations, media, hubs, switches, routers, printers, various types of servers, and other shared service devices.

LAN Devices

See LAN definition above

Lessons Learned

Lessons learned are those pieces of information gleaned experientially from the exercise of a plan. Lessons learned derived from plan's testing are an integral part of the "project life cycle" used to revise and improve a plan.

Life Cycle or Project Life Cycle

A project life cycle is a paradigm that has a beginning phase, a research phase, a design phase, an implementation phase, and an end phase. With the subsequent inclusion of "lessons learned" from testing, the plan is then revised and the "life cycle" starts all over again.

LLI = Long Lead Item

A long lead item is a task, an event, or perhaps a goal that the PM knows is going to take a long time to accomplish. LLIs are usually on the "critical path." Matters like real estate, telephony circuits, and equipment purchases are usually considered LLIs. Sometimes an organization's management will give permission to fund LLIs before the Implementation Phase begins but in anticipation that the LLI will be needed on a timely basis once the implementation is commenced.

Metric

The term "metric" is often used in project management and business as meaning "measurement"—especially as in the quantification of system inputs and outputs.

Migrations

Within a networked computer environment, the word "migration" represents the process of users moving from one place to another. See "Restacks."

Milestone

A milestone is a major event in a project plan. It is often used to describe the successful completion of an important objective.

MIS

MIS stands for management information systems. The MIS discipline focuses on the use of technology in the management of an organization.

MOP = Measure of Performance

Measures of performance elements are the items in the various metrics matrix. The MOPs must be compiled and analyzed to determine the success or failure of a project.

Off the Shelf

Hardware and software readily procured from vendor sources is said to be "off the shelf." This contrast with "in-house" built products that are often more expensive to develop in the long run. See also "Turn Key Solutions."

One-off Task

A one-off task is a task that does not fit the usual mold of departmental functions. Oftentimes, a legacy routine that has been inherited by the organization and never updated to current technology standards is considered a "one-off task."

Opportunity Cost

Opportunity cost is that monetary amount assessed for any reason against potential but unrealized earnings. The concept is used In DR/COB planning to express that amount of dollars that could potentially be lost to a disaster should a robust plan not be in place. Compare opportunity cost to "plan investment" to derive an ROI ratio.

Organizational Silos

The metaphor of a silo is used to describe an organization or part of an organization that conducts its business and communications in an insular manner. It passes information up and down its own organization but does not keep other corporate departments informed of its activities. This practice can be disadvantageous to efficient production.

PBX = Private Branch Exchange

The acronym PBX stands for private branch exchange. This device is an in-house telephone switch—usually installed and maintained by the local telephone company. The switch allows connectivity to telephone circuits and routing of telephone calls within and outside of the site.

PDS = Premises Distribution System

A PDS is a schema representing the electrical wiring at a site. It can sometimes also refer to the system of cables connecting the different elements of a LAN.

Pecking Order

The pecking order in an organization represents the hierarchy of authority. A project manager is wise to understand the pecking order to insure that issues can receive the proper attention from someone that has the authority to approve a solution.

NAS = Network Attached Storage

According to http://searchstorage.techtarget.com the definition of NAS is "storage that is set up with its own network address rather than being attached to the department computer that is serving applications to a network's workstation users." This arrangement increases the efficiency of response and throughput. An expanded NAS system is sometimes called a SAN or storage area network.

PC = Project Council or User Council

The PC is a group of people gathered from different departments. Headed by the PM, it meets to represent the organization for efficiently communicating information. It meets periodically and serves as a "board of directors" for the organization's project.

PCM = Process Control Manual

A PCM is a guide to BAU and emergency processes. Best practices in the form of standard operating procedures are stipulated within the PCM so that consistency of response to all situations can be achieved across the environment both local and global.

All technical information that might be needed regarding the technical conduct of the IT service team should be in the PCM. Copies should be kept on and off site.

The PCM is a dynamic document constantly updated in light of new situations, personnel or information. The PCM should be readily available to technicians when there is a question of how to proceed.

PDC = Primary Domain Controller

The primary domain controller hosts a database of the users and resources within a domain. Once authenticated, a user can connect to other file and print services on the same domain. BDC, or backup domain controllers, are replicates of the PDC and are used for redundancy. Other special domains called **resources domains** can be granted a trust relationship to the PDC so that the users authenticated to the PDC can access resources in the special domain.

PDLC = Project Development Life Cycle

The Project Development Life Cycle is similar to other life cycle paradigms. It cycles through discovery, design, and implementation in an iterative manner, using "lessons learned" to revise and improve the existing plan.

PDS = Premises Distribution System

The premises distribution system is the media (copper, fiber, wireless) and connecting apparatus (tech plates, multiplexers, etc.) that move the data packets from the workstation to the LAN backbone.

Primary Data Set

Differentiated from a backup data set, the primary data set is that data that represents the current working data. To prevent data corruption, users should never be allowed to use two separate "primary or working data sets" without an effective system to synchronize the two.

PM = Project Manager

A project manager is that individual who compiles a project plan and brings together a project team to gather information and collate design and implementation activities toward the completion of projects.

PP = Project Plan

A project plan is an logical arrangement of tasks, dates, time lines, milestones, critical path items, responsibility attributions, and budgetary information. Depending on the project and the PM, the PP can be relatively simple or very complex.

Remote Access

In the context of a DR/COB scenario, remote access means that a user can access primary or alternate network assets via a remote circuit. Sometimes COB workers are given the ability to work from home through the Internet.

Restacks

For most operations managers working in major commercial sites, restacking or the moving of a department from one place to another is a constant activity.

RFI = Request for Information

An RFI is similar to an RFP but is more preliminary in the decision-to-procure process. This information is generally not tremendously detailed as to how the product might fit into particular situation. RFIs are often used for vendor suitability comparisons.

RFP = Request for Proposal

A Request for Proposal is a document from a sponsoring organization to vendors. It solicits detailed features, benefits, and prices from vendors of particular products and services prior to a purchase decision.

Right Sizing

Right sizing simply means that the DR/COB plan should be sized appropriate to the particular organization and cost effective depending on the value of the data that is being protected. Right sizing reflects the concept of DR/COB not as a sunk cost but as an investment expecting a return.

Risk Deviation

A risk deviation is a "sign-off" by the organization's management stipulating that they understand a particular risk, do not wish to ameliorate the risk, and accept the responsibility if something untoward happens because of the risk.

Generally, a risk deviation accepted by any single department cannot exceed the scope of that department. Said another way, one department cannot accept a risk for the entire company. For example, a department manager in a large company cannot accept the risk inherent in not having an effective computer virus protection program installed on departmental PCs when an infection could spread through the entire network.

ROI = Return on Investment

ROI is the ratio of financial inputs of the project divided by financial outputs produced by the project. The idea is that the investment of money or resources in a project should return a profit or a benefit in excess of the cost. (ROI calculation template found at Figure 2.)

SAN = Storage Area Network

A storage area network is a remote data store location. It can host a primary data source or be used for data replication. Special software with redundant arrays of small drives, optical drives, and tapes are often used to hold this data repository.

Scope

As used in project management, "scope" means the specific range of tasks and goals stipulated in the business requirement document.

Server Farm

In a large business, the term "server farm" is sometimes used to describe a secure room with cabinets holding a plethora of data servers.

Single Point of Failure

A robust computing environment should not have any single device, circuit, or other integral part of the environment upon which the entire system depends. All single points of failure should be made redundant so that, if one part fails, another can take its place to maintain production.

SLA = Service Level Agreement

A service level agreement is a contract between a service organization and a client that defines the parameters of their relationship as they relate to the delivery of the vendor's service. Alacrity of response to particular situations and time to fulfillment of service requests are two elements of an SLA. The agreement can also stipulate how the quantity and quality of service delivery should be measured. It is common for an SLA to specify differential in payment to the vendor depending on the service metrics.

SOP = Standard Operating Procedures

Standard operating procedures are those activities and techniques that have been codified into organizational policy. A documented SOP is a reference for team members to follow. A well-designed and current SOP or PCM document will promote consistency and should allow a knowledge expert from another part of the organization to step in and perform BAU/DR or COB activities with a minimum of effort.

Staging

"To stage" a project or task is to procure and prepare sufficient space and resources to expedite completion.

Stakeholder

In project management parlance, stakeholders are those individuals that have a stake in or are impacted by the process or outcome of a project.

Stand-alone Device

A stand-alone device is one that is not connected to or dependent on the network.

Street Power

Street power is that electrical power provided by the local power company. It is prudent to have more than one power feed into a facility to accommodate failover. Because street power is oftentimes not reliable, electrical generators and uninterrupted power supplies are desirable to indemnify a critical network against power outages.

Team Lead

The term "team lead" may sometimes refer to a high-level project manager, or it can refer to the leader of a subordinate team.

Tech Plates

The term "tech plate" refers to the LAN connection boxes that are usually found under each workstation. The computing devices use a cable to connect to a tech plate port. The ports on the tech plates are hardwired through to the LAN switches and routers to allow the availability of LAN resources.

Tech Room or Technical Room

A "tech room" is a special, controlled space that contains LAN or WAN equipment for the computer network. The room is usually secured for only authorized personnel. Depending on what the room contains, terms like "wiring closet," "wire room," "server room," "enterprise room," etc., are used.

Telephony

Telephony is a term that describes the transmission of signals over telephone company circuits.

Test Beds

A test bed is a laboratory that contains an accurate representation of the DR/COB environment being tested. It includes computers, software, data, and connectivity elements that, when used by departmental users, prove that the DR/COB site and plan will be effective. Sometimes test bed computers will have VNC (virtual network connection) into a remote PC at a COB site to test productions routines via the COB machine. This is an efficient way to emulate the actual COB environment without staff having to drive to the remote COB site.

TI = Technology Infrastructure

Technology infrastructure is a catchall term that refers to the facilities, services, and installations needed for the functioning of communication networks.

Time is of the Essence

If an activity needs to be completed within a particular period as an integral part of a contract, the agreement should stipulate "time is of the essence."

Time Lines

Within a project plan, time lines refer to the time allotted to complete a task.

Turn-key Solutions

"Turn-key Solutions" are "off-the-shelf" purchases provided by vendors. The functionality of these products have already been developed and tested. However, even if these products are touted as ready to go, it is not unusual that turnkey solutions need tweaking to fit ino unique situations.

UPS = Uninterrupted Power Supply

A UPS is a device that supplies instantaneous voltage from batteries to connected devices so that they are not affected by street power outages. The downside to a UPS is that the battery power rarely lasts (depending on the load) beyond thirty minutes. In large, critical organizations, a UPS is often connected to an electrical generator(s) that will commence power generation within several seconds after street power is lost. The electrical generator obviates the need to worry about the duration of battery power. However, one must now worry about the sufficiency of the fuel for the generator.

User Profiles

User profiles describe the data elements that allow a worker to be functional at their computer workstations. They are also created, recorded, and replicated at alternate workstations, so when a user logs on he or she can receive appropriate applications, data, and other LAN/WAN links that may be necessary.

WAN = Wide Area Network

A wide area network connects communication devices and networks over an area that is more extensive that a single or co-located facility. Within an Intranet, a WAN usually includes a long haul carrier in the chain of connectivity. For example, the Internet is a very wide area network.

"What if" Mind-set

The "what if" mind-set is an attitude that constantly questions the processes and infrastructure within a network environment toward the goal of discovering any single point of failure" or other anomaly that might present a danger to production.

Zero Defects

Originally adapted by Martin Marietta Corporation in Denver, Colorado, the term "zero defects" was first conceived by Philip Crosby in his Fourteen-Step Quality Improvement Process. It stipulated that adapting a no-mistakes quality control policy would lead to greater efficiency, be monetarily quantified, and enhance profits.

Sources of COB/DR Information

A review of disaster recovery literature and research produced many references to government DR plans for weather and geological catastrophes. Grand disaster plans seemed to be most numerous—followed in number by academic records, library preservation, IT company publications, and then non-vendor books. A significant amount of DR/COB planning literature found on the Internet represented professional IT companies that sell DR/COB products and consulting services to organizations. This literature often focused around particular product solutions.

In addition to vendor-solution-based, commercial-oriented literature, there are some excellent books for sale that focus on DR for computer networks and COB for organizations—both local and global. The available literature illustrates writing intended for different audiences by authors from different backgrounds.

Because this workbook was written mostly from the experiential activities of the author, other topical sources are highly recommended as an adjunct to this guide.

Other than the sources listed below in the bibliography and references section, the author suggests that a much more complete result of the available literature can be produced by simply using one of the popular Internet search engines to search for key phrases such as "disaster recovery," "continuity of business," "contingency planning," and other combinations of similar words.

Notable is the plethora of relevant books that are carried by Amazon.com.

Bibliography and References

1. Hiatt, Charlotte J. (2000). *A Primer for Disaster Recovery Planning in an IT Environment.* Idea Group Publishing. http://www.rothstein.com/drjbooks/drj458.htm.

2. Hiles, Andrew (2003). *Business Continuity: Best Practices—World-Class Business Continuity Management*, second Edition. Rothstein Associates Inc. http://www.rothstein.com/data/dr725prom.htm.

3. Wallace, Michael, and Lawrence Webber (2004). *Disaster Recovery Handbook, A Step-by-Step Plan to Ensure Business Continuity and Protect Vital Operations, Facilities, and Assets.* American Management Association. http://www.amanet.org/books/catalog/0814472400.htm.

4. Natural Hazards Research and Applications Information Center (2001). *Holistic Disaster Recovery, An annotated bibliography*, University of Colorado. http://www.colorado.edu/hazards/holistic_recovery/bib_2.html.

5. Info-Tech Research Group (2005). *Are you prepared if disaster strikes?* http://www.infotech.com/Products_and_services/Consulting/Methodologies/Disaster Recovery.

6. Sullivan, Tom (12/01/2000). **"Bracing for disaster.**" *InfoWorld Magazine.* http://www.infoworld.com/articles/su/xml/00/12/04/001204surecovery.html.

7. Erbschloe, Michael (2003). "Understanding the Disaster Recovery Planning Process." *IT Employment Advisors, An Internet Journal for Information Technology Professionals and Managers*, St. Louis Metro Edition, March 2003 Issue Vol. 1. No. 3. http://www.itemploymentadvisors.com/Articles/ITEA-Art2-0303PV.htm.

8. Erbschloe, Michael, and John Vacca, (March 10, 2003), Guide to Disaster Recovery. Course Technology.

9. Praxium Research Group Ltd. (2005).
   ISO 9001 2000 Gap Analysis Tool. http://www.praxiom.com/iso-gap.htm.

10. Microsoft Corporation (2005). *Discover Project 2003.* Office online.
    http://office.microsoft.com/en-us/FX010857951033.aspx.

11. State Records, New South Wales (June 2002). *Guidelines on Counter Disaster Strategies for Records and Recordkeeping Systems.*
    http://www.records.nsw.gov.au/publicsector/rk/guidelines/counterdisaster/Single-download.htm
    http://www.records.nsw.gov.au/publicsector/rk/guidelines/counterdisaster/Response.htm.

12. TrainingReviews.com (2005). *Training Reviews, Security: Disaster Recovery: Disaster Recovery Training.* http://www.trainingreviews.com/Detailed/216.html.

13. *The Technology of Disaster Recovery* (October 9, 2003). Veritas Corporation: http://www.veritas.com/van/articles/3943.jsp.

Index

A

Adds moves and changes, 24, 10
Agenda
    curtail digressions, 51
    form, 65
    hidden, 52
    include questions period, 50
    item time allotted - schedule, 10, 51
    meeting, 10
    publish, 50
    take charge, 51
    templates, 10, 13
Alert pyramid, 37, 66, 68, 76
    alternate persons, 36
    construction, 36
    definition, 110
    include communication devices, 36
    metric, 66
    test summary, 66, 67
    contact test metrics worksheet, 69
    contact sheet sample form, 68
All clear, 41
Antivirus, 29
Appropriate authority, 21, 48
As built, 105, 106, 111
Attribution, 111
    CAP (corrective action plan), 32
    expense, 89
    project planning template, 85, 87, 120
    task list, 12, 13
Automated system, 32
Awareness DR/COB, 74
    Situational, 3

B

Back out plan, 20
BAU, 112
    See Business As Usual
    SOP (standard operating procedure), 123
    support during DR project, 20
    PCM (process control manual) inclusion, 119
Best of breed, 28
Best practice, 112
    discover solutions, 12, 88
    PCM (process control manual), 32, 119
    planning for the worst, XI
    reliability, 28
    team building - leadership skills, 57
Bibliography and references, 127, 129
Bill Lin, PhD, VI
Bill of materials, 112
    See BOM
Bit level Replication, 19
BOM, 91, 98, 100, 112
    create, 90
    sample, 100
BRD, 13, 91, 112
Break and fix, 24, 112
Build, 111, 112
Build
    parallel, 18
    elevations, 115
    engage specialists, 3
    "as built" document, 105
    installation of equipment, 14
    project budget, 55
    project time lines, 106

servers, desktops - ghosted, 62, 94, 95, 96
site considerations, 88
sufficient space, 91
task lists, 13
Business as usual, 20, 112
See BAU
Business impact analysis, 32
Business location, 72, 75
Business Managers, XII, I
explain ROI (return on investment), 55
review user profiles, 91
stakeholders, 9
information form, 70
Business requirement document, 13, 54, 88, 122

C

Cabinets, 91, 93, 94, 103, 115, 122
Circuit, 90, 120, 122
telephony, 14
facility entry points, 60
parts of a WAN (wide area network) circuit, 60
redundant, 30, 59, 60, 61
WAN (wide area network) needs, 15, 28
Classic project management, 5, 7, 25, 46, 47, 57
Client
host, 42, 115
server, 42, 89
Close, 7, 10, 18, 23, 47, 88, 97, 99, 102
Closure, 106
Clusters of Rs, 27, 37, 44
CNDA (*Confidential Nondisclosure Agreement*), 9
See Confidential Nondisclosure Agreement
CO (central office)
See telephone company
Collective solutions, 48
Communications
insular silos, 118
issues, 36
solution for technophobia, 56
close the Loop, 10
destruction, 36
mobile devices, 36
more than one methodology, 36, 66
Project Council, 9
matrix, 10, 11, 89
Complexity, 31, 46
Conceptual Elements of a COB/DR Plan, 4
Confidential Nondisclosure Agreement, 9, 113
See CNDA

Construction checklist for technical equipment areas (partial), 103
Consultants
advantages, 9
FTEs (full time equivalents), 116
temp to permanent, 9
temporary - at will help, 9
Contents, xiii
Continuity of business
COB Verses DR, 3
definition, 113
various departments, 84
Coordinator alternates form (COB/DR), 71
Coordinators form (COB/DR), 71
Cost
expand for project scope increase, 54
generous estimates, 54
Level I Estimate, 9
Level 3 Estimate, 3
of failure, 2
opportunity, 31, 42
unnecessary, 46
and benefit, 42, 46
assessment spreadsheet, 106
effectiveness, 29
verses investment, 55
Critical
business processes, I, 28
DR/COB question, What if..?, 2
files, 19
Path Items (CPI), 12, 49, 113
Path Items In project plan, 120
stakeholders, 37
subsets of processes, 16
Cross train staff, 62
Crosshatched
redundant - failover, 60
WAN circuits, 60
Customer Satisfaction
form for the IT Team, XV, 108
survey, 23

D

Dark Space, 18, 73
Data restoration, 19
time line, 61, 62
Decision
bottlenecks, 21
maker, 8, 49

maker purse strings, 3
Declaration of emergency, 36, 39
Declare emergency, 17, 33
Definition of
   terms, 110
   success MOP (measure of performance), 117
Delegate responsibility, 45, 51
Deliverables, 4, 10, 27, 71, 98, 114
   burnout, 21
   project checklist, 42, 106
Demarc or d-mark, 94, 103, 104, 114, 116
Dependencies, 53, 66, 87, 114
   compiling, 11
   human factors, 39
   prioritize, 53
   task list, 12
Deploy, train, test, revise, 43
Deportment, 22
Design, 8, 24, 43, 88, 90, 91, 92, 93, 94, 106, 120
   accomplishes function, 1
   "as built" documents, 111
   brainstorming, 32
   complete solution, 29
   cooperation, 2, 14
   cost estimates, 16
   critical subset, 16
   hot cutover, 18
   level 3 cost estimate, 62
   orderly deployment, 20
   part of project life cycle, 47
   phased approach, 16
   professional design help, 9
   scope creep, 48
   sponsor commitment, 11, 13
   testing, 3, 15
   time line, 99
   uses discovery information, 16
   phase, 7, 9, 13, 15, 16, 42, 117
Detailed project plan template - sample #3, 88
Disaster
   alert contact pyramid test guidelines, 66
   insurance, 40
   levels, 16
Disaster Recovery DR, 43
   approach, 25
   backout plan, 20
   COB (continuity of business), 113, 114
   contacting stakeholders, 66
   dark site, 114
   different severities, 17

encryption, 34
focus of workbook, 4
how to avoid it, 29
how to communicate it, 36
impact on personnel, 5
Integration of DR and COB, 3
law of inertia, 56
an insurance policy, 1
literature, 127
opportunity cost, 118
parallel production, 28
phased plans, 39
plan results and deliverables, 42
project management approach, 57
publish plan with care, 35
restoration of primary environment, 41
reversing plan actions, 41
revision training, 37
right sizing, 31
risk acceptance, 75
risk level, 33
single point of failure, 59
stay calm, 22
survival of workers, 27
test planning worksheet, 78
training, 4
where to gather, 37
who will decide, 36
wishful thinking, 46
plan type checklist, 74, 44
Discovery
   opportunity cost estimate, 31
   agreement with implementation
      activities, 32
   check discovery questionnaire, 13
   cooperative effort, 2
   discovery phase, 15, 22, 88
   get a sponsor, 8
   hot buttons, 116
   level 3 cost estimate, 62
   loss of production tolerance, 32
   PDLC (project development life cycle), 120
   preliminary ROI (return on investment), 9
   project methodology, 7
   project plan template, 89
   remote site, 69
   scope creep, 48
   single points of failure, 44
   solid sponsor commitment, 11
   use the project council, 11

use to discover importance of functions, 16
using interrogation of users, 11
questionnaire, 13
Distance matrix form COB/DR, 72
Documentation
  "as built", 111
  location, 86
  need for, 1
  project plan template, 95, 97
  test results, 81
Down time, 2, 32, 115
DR/COB
  concepts associated with a cluster of Rs, 27
  remote site planning Form, 69
  test planning worksheet form, 76
  test results form, 79
DSU (digital service unit), 80, 91, 92, 94
Dummy data sets, 16
Dynamic document
  communications matrix, 10
  inventory, 15
  PCM (process control manual), 119
  project plan is a, 4

E

Electric generator, 61
Employee considerations, 40
Emulator
  3270, 90
  session files, 30, 115
  Scripts, 72, 73, 90
Encrypted, 34
Encryptor, 90, 92, 94
Engagement
  authority, 48
  communications matrix, team building, 10
  cost, 31
  goals, 11
  level 3 cost estimate, 62
  looking for staff and stakeholders, 9
  project management phase, 7
  project plan template, 88
  scope and constraints, 8
Engagement, Pre-
  authority, 48
  Project Management Phase, 7
  project plan template, 88
  test the water, 8

Ethical, 56
Ethics, XIV, 45
Existing COB/DR recovery site locations
  form, 70

F

Facilitator, 65
Facility maintenance, 2
Failover, 60, 123
Fail-safe, 32
Failure to test and revise existing plans, 3
False sense of security, 3
Feasibility analysis and assessment, 8, 9
Financial
  impact of failure-basic form, XIV, 64
  resources, 40
Firewall, 29, 90, 115
"First - do no harm", 35
"First things first", 16, 39
Forewarning, 31
Forms and checklists, 13, 59, 69
FTE (full time equivalents), 63, 116
Full time equivalents (FTE), 63, 116
Functionality matrix form COB/DR, 72
Funding, 13, 20, 55

G

Gantt chart, 12
Gap analysis
  citation, 130
  cost, 32
  definition, 13
  path to completion, 32
  project template, 94, 97
Generator
  with UPS, 125
  uninterrupted power, 61
Ghosted, 62
Gossip, 3

H

Homework, 52
Hot Cutovers, 17, 18
Housekeeping, 10, 12
Hub and spoke decision bottlenecks, 21
Hubs, 60, 63, 116

I

Impediments, I, 13, 33
    to a workable DR/COB plan, I
Implementation
    BOM (bill of materials), 100
    cooperation with stakeholders, 46
    coordination, 14
    funding available, 20
    life cycle, LLI (long lead item), 117
    overlooked considerations, 43
    PDLC (project development life cycle), 120
    post or after, 22, 23, 24
    project plan template, 88, 91, 93, 94,
        95, 97
    staging space, 14
    test worksheet, 76
    time lines, 99
    time to execute, 39
    use of test beds, 15, 120
    phase, 7, 20
Incompetent, 50
Individual blame, 48
Integrity
    process and data, 16, 34, 40, 41
    personal, 45
Introduction, XVII
Inventory list, 40
Is it really necessary, 16
Is it worth it, 16
Iterations, 3

L

LAN [Local Area Network]
    hot cutovers, 18
    identify needs, 15
    part of computing systems, 5
    PCM (process control manual), 23
    PDS (premises distribution system), 118
    bit-level, data replication procedure, 20
    critical spare parts available, 59
    cross train, 62
    definition, 115
    expert personnel, 14
    focus of workbook, 4
    project plan template, 88-97
    redundant circuits, 59
    ports, switches and hubs, 60

    reliability, 28
    single point of failure, 30
    sufficient capacity, 80
    throughput, 28
Law of inertia, 56
Law of unintended consequences, 35
Leadership, 39, 57
Lessons learned
    ask for feedback, 48
    chapter 4, 45
    definition, 116
    life cycle element, 117, 120
    metrics of activities, 17
    post-implementation review, 23
    project plan template, 97
    records lead to, 52
    systematically update, 4, 22, 37
    test and revise, 3
    test results form, 80
    transfer to different teams, 24
Level three cost estimate - sample form, 62
levels of catastrophe, 17
License keys, 62
Life cycle
    paradigm, 22, 46, 120
    plan, 47
LLI (long lead items), 13, 14, 117

M

Maintenance, I
    break and fix, 112
    circuit, 106
    data, 2
    documents, 111
    facility, 2
    LAN (local area network), 62
    metrics, 24
    ongoing expense, 63, 98
    operational personnel, 22
    operations efficiency, 24
    physical and logical systems, 28
    plan, 20, 43
    system, 23, 32
    team space, 24
    team, 24, 32
    phase, 7, 23, 24
Malcontents, 50
Malfeasance interpretation, 29

Meeting agenda with last meeting minutes - sample
   form, 65
Meetings
   archive minutes, 23
   efficient and effective, 10
   engagement phase, 10
   project deliverable, 11
   simplest template, 87
   take charge, 51
   write it down, 52
Methodology project plan template, 88-97
Metrics
   alert pyramid, 69, 110
   consequence of not having, 3
   define success, 48
   implement and regularize, 24
   Microsoft excel, 12
   MOP (measure of performance)
      definition, 117
   project plan template, 88-97
   quantify entities, 12, 43
   satisfaction survey, 23
   SLA parameters, 122
   test results form, 79
   test results to lessons learned, 37
Microsoft
   Excel
      ROI (return on investment) template, 31
      task list, 13
   Project task list - Gantt chart, 12
   Word project planning template, 87
      task list, 13
Migration
   definition, 117
   designs, 18
   hot cutover, 18
   in project plan, 88-97
   operational, 17
   parallel build, 18
   restoration, 41
   techniques, 19
Milestone
   definition, 117
   document, 101
   in project plan, 88-97
   part of task list, 12
   plan deliverables, 42
   project time lines, 106
   task list compilation, 49

Multiple
   plans, 39
   projects worksheet sample, 84

N

Negative
   behaviors, 48, 50
   effect on productivity migrations, 18

O

Offsite data backup checklist, 41
One-off tasks unique departmental tasks, 15
Opinion and advice lessons learned, 45
Opportunities
   brainstorming, 43
   during crisis, 48
Opportunity cost
   as investment, 55
   cost and benefits, 42
   definition, 118
   impact of failure form, 64
   ROI (return on Investment), 31
Organizational
   politics, 53
   procrastination, 4

P

Parallel
   build, 18
   computing environments verses hot cut over, 17
   production facility, 27
Password
   in project plan, 88-97
   safeguarding, 34
Patch
   crosshatching, 60
   in project plan, 88-97
   tech plate and panel ports, 60
PBX (Private Branch Exchange)
   definition, 118
   milestone document, 102
   redundancy, 60
   technical checklist, 103
PCM (process control manual)
   create, 23
   definition, 119

deliverable, 43
   system maintenance, 32
   test and maintain, 24
   SOP (standard operating procedure), 123
PDLC (project development life cycle)
   definition, 120
PDS (premises distribution system)
   construction checklist, 103
   definition, 118
   project plan, 88-97
Pecking order
   be aware, 53
   definition, 119
Personnel
   COB (continuity of business) attributes, 3, 6
   insufficient regard, 2
   issues, 18-19
   part of computing system, 5
   project plan, 88-97
   survival, 27
Plain old telephone line (POT), 68
Players, 49
   hot buttons, 50
PM (project manager)
   definition, 120
   responsibilities, 35, 51, 52, 53, 54, 57
   self view, 22, 56
Port activation, 60
Post-implementation phase, 33
Preface, XI
Premises distribution system
   See PDS
Primary data set
   avoid duplicate, 16, 41
   bit level data replication, 112
   definition, 120
   destruction, 19
Prioritize
   plans for severity, 38
   tasks, 53
Private Branch Exchange
   See PBX
Process function and design catalog production
   processes, 1
Project
   approach, 46
   completion and feedback-sample form, 106
   control Manual
      See PCM

council
   board of directors, 10
   communicating, 22
   create BRD (business requirement document), 13
   definition aka User Council, 119
   discovery phase, 11
   engagement phase, 9
   should include, 9
development life cycle
   See PDLC (project development life cycle)
management
   phases, 7
   life cycle
      See PDLC (project development life cycle)
manager (project manager) definition
   See PM (project manager)
methodology, 7
planning
   document-sample #4, 98
   milestone document-Sample #5, 101
   simplest template-Sample #2, 87
   template-sample #1, 85
records, 23
sponsor, 8, 47, 49
Proof of
   application license, 62
   concept testing, 15, 16
Psychological denial impediments to
   planning, 1
Publish
   available to stakeholders, 35
   metrics, 43
   project plan, 88-97
   to user base, 17
   update, 49
Purse string privileges
   decision maker, 3

Q

Quantifiable entities for metrics, 12

R

Ramifications, 35
Rapidity, 38
Reachable, 36
Reactive, 36

Readiness, 38
Ready, willing and able, 36
Real estate
    facility maintenance, 2
    long lead items, 14
Real time replication, 19, 20, 112
Reality, 27
Reasonable, 30
Reconnaissance, 31
Recuperation, 41
Redundancy, 30, 59
Refine, 37
Refrain, 37
Rehearse, 37
Relegation, 36
Relevant, 30
Reliability, 28
Remediable, 29
Remedial plans, 3
Remote
    location, 39, 42
    site, 14, 16, 19, 24
        at ready, 40
        dark site, 40
        distance, 39
        planning form, 69
Remoteness, 38
Replication, 30, 50
    bit level, 112
    off site, 33
    real time, 19
Request for information (RFI)
    definition, 121, 123
Request for proposal (RFP), 8, 10, 121
    definition, 121
    pre-engagement phase, 8
Resources
    alternate site, 41
    change in scope, 47, 48, 49
    commitment of, 43
    discussion of
    financial, 40
    prioritize, 53
    scarcity, 3
    sufficiency, 21, 51
Respect
    give to get, 56
    team time, 51
Responsibility, 36
    accepting risk, 121

delegating, 45, 51
Restacks, 121
    migrations, 117
Restoration, 41
    data backup machines, 19
    test data, 19
    time line, 19, 61
Restore
    object lesson, 38
    to primary site, 42
Results, 42
    lessons learned, 4
    measure, 3, 43
    test results form, 79
Resumption, 41
Retrain, 37
Return on investment (ROI)
    definition, 122
    financial justification, 8, 16, 33
    impact of failure form, 64
    use in presentations, 55
    do not exceed cost of failure, 2, 31
Reversibility, 41
Review, 37
    post implementation, 23
    project plan, 88-97
Revise, 37
    definition of life cycle, 116, 117
    failure to, 3
    test and rehearse revisions, 17, 37
Right sized, 30
Right sizing
    definition, 121
Risk
    acceptance for disaster plan deviations
        form, 75
    analysis, 32, 94
Robustness, 28
    redundancy, 30
    remediable, 29
ROI
    See Return on Investment
Roles, 36
    project plan, 89
    teambuilding, 11
Routers
    project plan, 88-97
    redundancy checklist, 60
Rules, 35
    ethics, 45

S

Scope
  limitations of this workbook, 4
  creep
    additional work, 49
    lessoned learned, 48
Server build
  project plan, 94
Service level agreement (SLA)
  definition, 122
Silos organizational, 21
  definition, 118
Single point of failure
  definition, 122
  redundancy, 30
  "what if" mindset, 125
Site survey
  project plan, 91
SLA
  See service level agreement
Software and application information collection form, 82
SOP
  See standard operating procedure
Sources of COB/DR
  information, 127
  maintenance, 24
  redundancy/replication checklist, 58
  remediable, 29
Special favors
  ethics, 45
Sponsor
  See project sponsor
Staging area
  housekeeping, 10
Stakeholders
  alert pyramid, 36, 66
  communications matrix, 10
  communications, 14, 50
  definition, 123
  engagement phase, 9
  negotiate with, 35
  planning template, 85, 87
  project
    council, 11
    plan, 88-97
Standard operating procedure (SOP)
  definition, 123
  in the PCM (process control manual), 43
Street power definition, 123

Subordinates
  boss works for, 56
  give respect, 56
  hub and spoke, 21
Summary of
  Chapter 1, 5
  Chapter 2, 25
  Chapter 3, 44
  Chapter 4, 57
  Chapter 5, 109
Switches
  project plan, 88-97
  redundancy, 60
Synchronized replication schema restoration, 41

T

Tape storage logs, 34
Target organization information form, 69
Team building, 57
  engagement phase, 11
Tech plates
  definition, 124
  PDS (premises distribution system), 120
  project plan, 88-97
  redundancy, 60
Tech room
  checklist, 103
  definition, 124
  POT (plain old telephone) line, 60
  project plan, 88-97
  redundancy, 61
Telephone Company (CO)
  WAN (wide area network) circuit parts, 60
  PBX (private branch exchange), 60
  project plan, 92
  telephony, 124
Test
  alert pyramid, 37, 66, 69
  different disaster levels, 16
  dummy data
  failure to, 3
  for unintended consequences, 35
  planning worksheet, 76 -77
  project plan, 88-97
  real world, 16
  restoration of data, 19
  results form
  staging, 10
  beds, 15, 124

Testing
  importance of, 4, 15, 24, 34, 38, 79
Thin clients, 42
Time lines
  definition, 125
  guard against, 54
  planning template, 85, 99, 106
  set for CAP (corrective action plan) resolution,
    32, 33
  submit as goals, 13
  visually with *MS (Microsoft) Project*, 12
Train
  cross train, 62
  failure, 4
  refrain cycle
  team building, 11
  checklist, 74
  use the PCM (process control manual), 32
  user and technician obligations, 17
Triage
  mechanism to select correct plan, 39
Tuckman
  stages, 57
  team building, 57

U

Unencrypted
  data, 34
Uninterrupted power supply (UPS), 61
  definition, 125
User
  data information collection matrix form, 83
  profiles
    definition, 125
    project plan, 88-97

stored off site, 62
updated, 62

V

Vendors
  don't be hoodwinked, 56
  engage, 10
  information and solutions, 28
  RFI (request for information), 121
  RFP (request for proposal), 121
  turnkey solutions, 125
Verbal agreement amnesia lessons learned, 49

W

WAN (Wide Area Network)
  BOM (bill of materials), 100
  definition, 125
  design needs, 15
  link to COB site, 16
  milestone document, 101-102
  NAS (network attached storage), 28
  project plan, 88-97
  redundant, crosshatched, 30, 60
  scope of book, 5
Wishful thinking
  lessons learned, 46
Work from home
  remote access solution, 40, 120

Z

Zero defects
  definition, 126
  parallel build, 18

www.ingramcontent.com/pod-product-compliance
Lightning Source LLC
Chambersburg PA
CBHW080419060326
40689CB00019B/4298